thor.

redneck way to
C.O.N.N.E.C.T. and make
your life be like God
intended it to be!

PATCHED WANGS

The Redneck Way to C.O.N.N.E.C.T. and Make Your Life Be Like God Intended It To Be!

BY AMANDA NELSON

PATCHED WANGS
St Petersburg, FL
USA

DISCLAIMER:

The author only shares true stories of herself and her family and what has worked for her to get sober from a drug and alcohol addiction. This book is not intended as a substitute for the medical advice of a professional. The reader should consult a physician in matters relating to his/her health, particularly with respect to any symptoms from alcohol or drug withdrawals that may require medical attention.

Editing and design by Sara Zibrat
Cover Photo by Kenneth Nelson

ISBN 978-0-692-88152-1
Library of Congress Cataloging Number: 2017906064

Publisher's Cataloging-In-Publication Data
(Prepared by The Donohue Group, Inc.)

Names: Nelson, Amanda (Amanda Paige), 1981-
Title: Patched wangs : the redneck way to C.O.N.N.E.C.T. and make
    your life be like God intended it to be! / by Amanda Nelson.
Description: St Petersburg, FL, USA : Patched Wangs, [2017]
Identifiers: LCCN 2017906064 | ISBN 978-0-692-88152-1
Subjects: LCSH: Recovering addicts--Religious life. | Drug addicts--
    Rehabilitation--Religious aspects. | Alcoholics--Rehabilitation--
    Religious aspects. | Christian life. | God (Christianity)--Will. |
    Happiness. | Nelson, Amanda (Amanda Paige), 1981---Drug use.
Classification: LCC BL625.9.R43 N45 2017 | DDC 204/.42--dc23

Patched Wangs
St. Petersburg, FL
www.patchedwangs.com
info@patchedwangs.com

TABLE OF CONTENTS

ACKNOWLEDGEMENTS

Without you, Alexis, I wouldn't be here today. To my "why," my daughter, thank you for giving me a reason to live.

Thank you, Dad and Turtle, for believing in me.

Thank you to my APOC family for sharing your testimonies of God's work and teaching me how to have a relationship with God.

Thank you to my Breathe University family for giving me a loving environment, where I could grow into the woman I was intended to be.

I want you to feel like you matter,
because you do.

WHY I WROTE THIS BOOK

I spent my 30th birthday in a traditional recovery center with approximately 40 women, learning the AA steps, and going to small group sessions. I went from living my life the way I wanted to, to living like a prisoner, almost. I spent 32 days living a very strict schedule. Breakfast, lunch, and supper were at a specific time each day. There were sign-up sheets taped to the wall to pick a time to shower. 10 minutes was all you got and if you wanted to shave your legs, a counselor had to be there with you to make sure you weren't about to cut yourself. Absolutely no privacy. We were only allowed to have 7 pairs of clothes with us; they were kept in a set of drawers in a room with 4 beds that was full of 4 women at all times. Our makeup had to be locked up at night and anything that contained any form of alcohol wasn't allowed (mouthwash, toothpaste, shampoo, etc.) I got to call home from a pay phone and was only allowed 5 minutes on certain days of the week. I felt alone, even with so many women around me. It was almost like having an extensive stay in jail, with a few more amenities.

When I was released back into the real world, I didn't leave there feeling super confident I had a good support system. I felt like, to them, I was just another number that went through the program. I didn't feel like they truly believed I would succeed. I never got a call saying, "Hey! Just wanted to make sure you were doing great. How are you?" I felt like I was in the very same mental and emotional spot I was in when I went in there. NO ONE CARED, so why should I?

So I went back to drinking and using again and spent another 4 years in my addiction. It is true what they say: When you quit for a while and then go back to drinking and using, it's 10 times worse. I think it's because we try harder than ever to numb the pain. You can be addicted to lots of different things; my addiction just happened to be drugs and alcohol. To me, addiction is filling a void with a certain substance or action because you feel a disconnect somewhere in your life.

Looking back at my 16-year-old-self taking that first drink, all I wanted was to be loved. The moment the alcohol entered my body, I felt as if it gave me the biggest bear hug ever. It said "I love you Amanda!" and I said, "I love you back! So much!" I didn't know that I would be in this love/hate relationship for 17 years of my life.

When I ended up on Meth and hit rock bottom, my drug dealer looked me in the eyes one day and said "You were born to do great things, Amanda. You are too beautiful to be wasting your life away on this mess." I took his words to heart. Out of all of the people in this world that believed in me, this was the very person that had seen me at the absolute lowest point in my life.

What did he possibly see in me that I never saw in myself? He never saw me at my greatest. He saw a broken girl who had potential, because he saw past all my mistakes. He saw past all my flaws. For a moment, he saw the true Amanda that was buried deep down, under all the years of drug/alcohol abuse. It felt amazing to have someone believe in me, because for so long so many people had called me worthless.

Three days after that conversation, I had to make one of the biggest decisions of my life. I chose to fight for my life. I knew the road ahead wasn't going to be easy, but somehow—deep down—I knew it had to be done. I didn't know how I was going to do it and sometimes that's the scariest part.

I already knew what *didn't* work for me; now I just had to figure out what *did*. I didn't know where to start, but I had to take my focus off it all and just *do* stuff. Over the course of my sobriety, I came up with principles that I apply daily. They help keep me sober and I want to share them ALL with you. The good news is everyone can live a joyful, vibrant, SOBER life. We all just need a little direction.

I wrote this book to help guide those folks that have tried over and over again to make it to that one-year sobriety milestone. You may be like I was: I could never stay sober for more than a couple months at a time. I think we all just want to be loved and accepted, and I want to create that loving, encouraging environment that you need, but may have never seen before. I never knew how much I needed that love and support until I finally got it.

No matter how bruised, no matter how broken, no matter how wounded you may feel, you are beautiful/handsome and you deserve the best, just as much as anyone else in this world. I want you to feel like you matter, because you do. I want to be that person cheering you on just like someone did for me. I'm not an expert in this area, but I was broken for so long and I found a solution to my addiction.

Y'all know I can't keep it a secret. I know if these simple principles work for me, they will work for you, too. I promise to be honest and transparent, so you can grow from my failures and triumphs. I need a favor from you, though: Please make a commitment to yourself that you will finish this book and apply these principles for a minimum of 30 days. Each day, take little baby steps towards being the best version of you. And if you feel so much better within those 30 days, keep going. Don't stop. This is going to be a new lifestyle. It's not something you can do for just a few days and be done. If you really want to change and you really want to be happy, it's going to take action every single day—a lifestyle change—for the rest of your life. I BELIEVE IN YOU and I know one thing's for sure... IF I CAN DO THIS, SO CAN YOU!

I should mention that I will refer to you, the readers of this book, as Lil Babies because I want to nurture you back into the person you were born to be. It's my term of endearment. Y'all know that southern women have pet names for everyone!

My Prayer For You!

Dear Lord,

I thank you so much for leading your son/daughter to read this book. Thank you for giving them another chance at life! Thank you for breaking their chains! I'm asking you to give them the strength and the courage to overcome this addiction, Father. I'm claiming from this day forward that their life will be filled with joy and happiness, no matter what circumstances they face. Please open their minds and their hearts to receive the message and lessons they are about to read. IN JESUS' MOST HOLY NAME, AMEN! AMEN! AMEN!

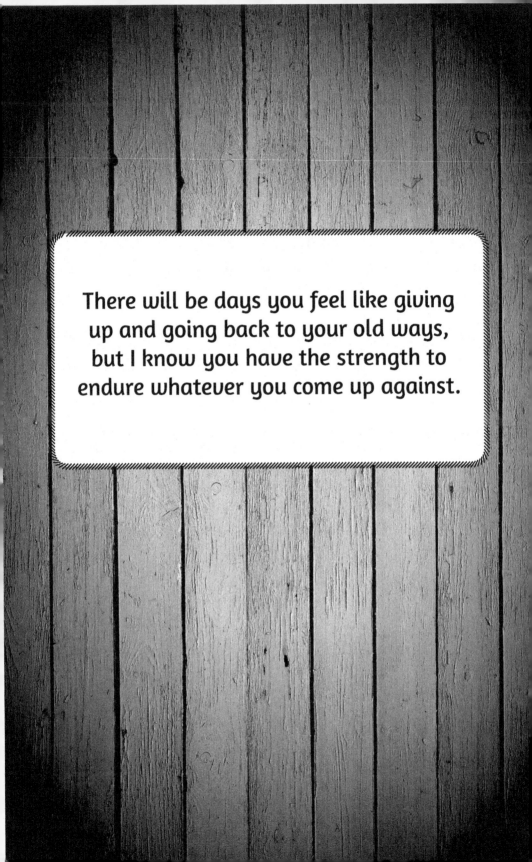

There will be days you feel like giving up and going back to your old ways, but I know you have the strength to endure whatever you come up against.

PAST PAIN, FUTURE GAIN

When I was in my addiction, I never felt like I was I was terminally ill. I never viewed it as a disease. Honestly, I didn't even know *what* to think of it until I got sober and started doing some research. I believe that addiction is a result of being disconnected from God, from the true version of you, your purpose, and love. I've heard Oprah say on many occasions that everyone just wants to be loved and accepted. It's so true. I was always searching for love and acceptance in the wrong places; I didn't understand that the only love that truly mattered was from God. As a result of not understanding this, I spent 17 years fueling my body with poisons and damaging relationships left and right.

I want to take you on a journey with me—my road to sobriety. I'm going to share with you some true stories that led me to where I'm at today. I've used the acronym C.O.N.N.E.C.T. as part of the name of this book because I truly believe that, once you connect yourself to love in some simple ways, you will be so filled up, you won't have any room for any bad addictions. We are going to create some new healthy ones! I'm so excited for your potential growth, I can't hardly stand it.

I would like to start by giving you an overview of my life in addiction, so that you will know I talk from experience and not just from something I watched on TV. This is by no means my whole story, but I feel it's necessary to highlight a few life-changing moments where my addiction had some serious impact.

2015 started off like a dad-gum country song. Yep! Get that knee slappin' jingle in your head. I lost a job, totaled my car, got evicted, and my dog died (all within a matter of weeks) because my addiction led me to Meth. I was only using it for about 10 months, but that drug destroyed my life so fast! I got arrested for the 4th time while I was on it, and that one happened to be a felony charge that I'm still trying to take care of to this day. Over all the years in my addiction, I swore to myself I'd never ever do that stuff again. I always thought it was a trailer trash drug, but there comes a point where nothing will fill that void and you just keep searching for something stronger and more potent. I felt disgusting while I was on it. I lost so much weight. I always felt like people were following me. I'm talking about super paranoia, kicked into overdrive. I kept thinking, "How did I get here? I used to have my life in order." Well, when seen from the outside, at least.

Like I said, I started drinking when I was 16. My parents divorced when I was about 4. Honestly, I didn't think it had any effect on me while I was growing up, but I'm learning that it impacted my life more than I had thought. My little brother and I lived with my mom and went to my dad's every other weekend. So basically, this was all I knew. Growing up, though, I never felt like I could measure up to what either one of them expected, especially my mom. For some reason, I always felt like she hated me. Maybe she was experiencing her own pain and she just didn't know how to cope with it. I'm not sure, but I just wanted that amazing mother and daughter relationship you always see in the movies. I never got it. It seemed like we were always arguing about something, no matter how hard I tried My junior year of high school, I changed schools for the second time. The first time was going into 6th grade, when my mom remarried. That was a hard transition in itself, but this time my mom kicked me out and made me go live with my dad. He didn't live in the same school district, so here we go again! But luckily for me, I already knew some people there and immediately gravitated towards the party crowd.

The night I took that first sip, I seriously felt like I had just met the love of my life. I didn't know it at the time, but it would be just like a relationship—a very damaging, controlling one, but I thought that's what love felt like. When you went to parties in high school, do you remember that one girl who was always sloppy wasted? The one who was always falling all over the place, the one who ALWAYS threw up? You know exactly who I'm talking about. That girl was me. It was never intentional, but somehow I always ended up like that. I was always the one everyone got mad at because of it, but I didn't care; I felt loved by the beer.

I wanted more of that feeling, so I decided to have an "open relationship" and invite drugs into the mix. Of course, I was like everyone else and started smoking weed. And then I just wanted to be messed up all the time. I tried Meth for the first time in high school and somehow, I knew deep down that it would be the very thing that destroyed me. It's amazing how much my intuition was talking to me even then, but I almost never listened. I did, however, listen to it on this particular thing and I never did Meth again until many, many years later

During my senior year of high school, I got arrested twice. I was fortunate enough not to spend any length of time in jail. I just had a look at my transcripts the other day, and I can tell exactly when I started my addiction because my grades started falling dramatically. Every day after lunch, I just left school, completely ignoring my last two classes. If my dad hadn't gone to the school to talk to them, I wouldn't have been able to graduate. By this time I was using ecstasy, acid, pills, weed... really, whatever I could get my hands on. At one time I could've been voted most likely to succeed, but not anymore. I just wanted to get the heck out of that place.

Right after high school, I decided to move to Florida to get a fresh start, but there was a problem: I was still hanging out with the same kind of people. There's no way I had a chance of changing. I ended up getting pregnant and getting married at the age of 19. That marriage didn't even last a year. We were so young and there was so much hatred. He was verbally abusive and super controlling. He never physically laid a hand on me, but I'd been isolated from my family and from the world. He got super jealous anytime I wanted to get out of the house and was always accusing me of cheating on him. I wasn't allowed to get a job because I was commanded to stay at home and raise the baby. People from the outside don't really understand what it's like to be in a situation like that. They say, "Well, just leave." It's a seriously terrifying experience, especially when you don't know how the dude will react if you do leave. Threats and screams of how worthless I was always played in my head when he was there and even when he wasn't. I was terrified to make a wrong move in my own home. I didn't ever want to do anything to set him off. I was still just wanting to be loved, but I knew deep down this isn't real love. This isn't what it's meant to be like.

When I finally mustered up the courage to leave him, it came with a price. He didn't want anything to do with our daughter. So here goes love again, on so many different levels. . I desperately wanted someone just to love me with open arms, without any arguing or yelling involved, and the one guy that said he *did* really didn't. To top it all off, he chose not to be a father figure. That broke my heart into 5 jillion pieces.

I will never forget the day after I moved back to Mississippi, working on the teller line at the bank. He called me at work just to tell me how much he hated me and that he didn't want anything to do with MY daughter. Now it wasn't even *our* daughter; he referred to her as MY daughter. I must've been sobbing so loud, because my manager came and pulled me off the teller line and sent me home for the day. I was humiliated. I felt so alone. How was I going to show love to my daughter when I didn't even feel it for myself? The drinking didn't stop, but somehow I found the strength to provide for us. I thought I did a decent job with what I had to work with.

I never thought I had a problem because I was still going to work and still taking care of my daughter. The years went on, and the drinking got worse. I had to take pills and uppers during the day to keep myself awake after drinking all night. It was a vicious cycle. Relationship after relationship went by, and the more I felt unloved, the more I turned to drugs and alcohol. 2010 was probably the year that I had that "I think I may really have a problem" moment, but there was absolutely no way I could admit that to anyone. It seemed as if that was the year that bad things happened to me back to back to back: I had a run-in with Child Protective Services while visiting Florida; I had an emergency surgery due to an ectopic pregnancy (that caused internal bleeding), another miscarriage about 4 months after that, an abusive relationship that landed me in jail for domestic violence (I spent 36 hours in the county jail), and then finally, my parents did an intervention and threw me in rehab. I was so depressed and angry at all of this that was happening. I didn't understand what I'd done that was so horrible to deserve all of this. Emotionally, I was a wreck. But the more I hurt, the more I wanted to numb it all.

I got sober for a few months. Two of them, I was forced to because I was in a facility. I felt so alone. I felt like no one understood what I went through. Instead of trying to figure out how I was feeling, people just judged me and pointed fingers at me. I wanted just one person to seem like they cared and try to help me get to the bottom of it. The truth is, I was hurting so bad on the inside, but I had to be tough on the outside, because that's what everyone thought I was for so long. I tried so hard to please everyone because I was searching for that love and acceptance, but in doing that, I sacrificed my own happiness, which made me drink and use even more. I knew deep down I belonged back in Florida, but I never went because my family didn't want me to go. The longer I stayed in Mississippi, the worse things got.

When I was sober for those few months, I didn't replace that void with anything. I just let it be there. I've since learned that when something is removed from you, it has to be replaced with something else. It can't just be empty space; it doesn't work like that. After a few weeks of being sober, no one seemed to care or encourage me or really find out why I was in the state I was in, so back to drinking I went. At first, it started as one beer here or there, because "I had it under control." It's kind of like the Pringles commercial, "Once you pop, you can't stop." I couldn't handle just one, because I was still dealing with so much pain deep down. I was drinking cases of beer by myself with or without others around. I never wanted to leave a single beer in the fridge. They all had to be drank up that night. That sounds like some dumb reasoning to me now, but that's the way it was. There were so many nights that beer was my supper. I made sure to cook my kiddo something to eat and there would be plenty for me, but I never ate it. I just drank my calories, so you can imagine how I was starting to look.

A lot of the last four years of my addiction were a blur, because I'd finally reached a point that I honestly didn't care if I lived or died. My daughter and I were fighting constantly. One day, I walked out of the job that I'd had for a couple of years because I didn't like my boss's rules. I just left. How dumb was that? That pattern continued on through two more jobs after that.

I'd been taking Aderol® for a while. It's a medication they prescribe to those with ADD, but if you don't have ADD, it makes you speed up instead of slow down. I had to have something keep me awake from the drinking all night. One day, there was none to be found in my home town. The next move after that was Meth. I knew deep down I shouldn't even go there, but I was so desperate for something to keep me awake, I didn't care anymore about how people would look at me. Even *I* couldn't stand to look at the girl I saw in the mirror anymore.

I got my first felony arrest just weeks after I started using Meth and was charged with embezzlement I had to fuel my addiction, so I stole checks from my employer and made them out to myself. I'm not sure why I thought I would never get caught. I guess it was because, deep down, I knew I was a good person, but the day I got arrested, I embarrassed my whole family. I had to experience the shame of knowing that I had let my parents down. My dad and stepmom own two businesses in the town I got arrested in, so now they looked like idiots because their daughter can't get it right. Man, that's the worst feeling in the world! Luckily, I only spent a few minutes in jail before the bondsman came and got me. And then it was right back to life, like nothing really happened. I did get sentenced with pre-trial diversion, since it was my first felony offense. As long as I paid the restitution plus all the associated fines, I wouldn't have a conviction on my record. I'm still paying on this today.

After my arrest, my daughter decided to go stay with my parents for a few weeks, which turned into a few months. The little girl that I'd raised by myself all those years and made so many sacrifices for didn't want to live with me anymore because I worshipped this addiction above everything else, including her. I cared more about finding my next high, not because I loved it anymore, but because I didn't feel like I had any other option. I had fallen out of love with alcohol and drugs a long time before.

It wasn't fun anymore. I wasn't laughing and joking around anymore. I was a Meth head. I lost a bunch of weight. Seriously, I looked so sick! It seemed like the more pain I tried to numb, the more pain stacked up on top of that pain. I lost everything in such a short period of time, including my dignity.

Mother's Day 2015 was a day I will never forget for the rest of my life. After I got evicted from my house, my good buddy let me stay at his house for a few months. After another attempt at a job and failing again, my hopes for myself were just about nonexistent. On that Mother's Day, my daughter was going to come hang out with me, but I was wallerin' in my own self-pity so much that she put my present on the floor, ran out of that house, and slammed the door. I can only imagine what that little girl was feeling in that moment. She still loved me enough to bring me a present, but I was so depressed and so hurt—almost to the point of no return, because that day I wanted to die. I wanted to end my life right then. I didn't think I had anything to live for. Something inside me made me go get some more Meth with the little bit of money that I had left. That's the day drug dealer spoke life into me. And I was desperate enough to believe everything he said. That's the day I'd waited on for so long... for one person to believe in me. I still find it ironic that it was the dope man, but hey! I know that in that moment, he was placed in my life to save my life.

Three days after that conversation, with only $200 in my pocket (and I got *that* by trading my dad my food stamps for some cash, which I do not recommend because it is illegal, but I told you I was going to be honest), I loaded up all I could in my car and started driving to Florida. I hadn't been down there in years and honestly didn't have a plan, but I knew if I didn't leave Mississippi right then, I would either end up in prison or dead. I had to leave my family behind, including my daughter, and it broke my heart so much, but I knew this is what I had to do to get my life back. I reached out to some folks I hadn't talked to in quite a number of years, and one was gracious enough to allow me to live on their boat for a while. When I first moved down, I'd let go of the Meth and picked up the drinking again. I eventually got a job and a place of my own to live. Man, getting the keys to my own place again felt so good! I felt like I was climbing back up, but I was still hanging on to my first love... alcohol!

(The parts I remember about my last date with alcohol are still so clear in my mind, but you know what? I'm going to save that story for another chapter. I want to explain it with an important principle that I learned and it fits better there.)

I was tired of living this life. I was tired of this constant cycle. I was tired of being unhappy. I was mentally, physically, and emotionally drained. Plum exhausted. I finally was where I'd wanted to be for so long, back in Florida. Now it was time to get my act straight. I had to! I had a little girl that was waiting for her mama to be present in her life again. August 10, 2015 was the day I laid it all down. Drugs, alcohol, cigarettes, and Coca-Cola®. I'm an "all or nothing" kind of person, so I figured, "If I'm going to do this, I'm going to do it right." From that day on, I decided to live in a 24-hour period, meaning that I couldn't worry about the days and weeks ahead; I had to just focus on the day I was living in.

In my first year of sobriety, I discovered a lot about myself. I found an inner strength that I never knew I had. If someone would've told me ahead of time about all that I would face while I was on a mission to get sober, I'm not sure I would've done it, but the good news is that no one told me, so I just walked in faith and trusted that everything I experienced was necessary to get me where I'm at today. I found a set of principles that helped me get from being a severely-broken girl to the happy young woman I am today. I believe that if you focus on the solution (and not the problem) each day and change your perspective on how you see things, then you won't have any other option but to live a joyful life. There will be days you feel like giving up and going back to your old ways, but I know you have the strength to endure whatever you come up against.

I live by these principles. If for some reason, I have a day where I feel weak, I ask myself, "Have I fed my Mind, Body, and Soul today?" I have a routine I do before I even start my day and I suggest you do the same, so you can be prepared to face whatever the day may bring. Your addiction could be food, TV, gambling—there's so many out there, I can't possibly name them all. I believe these principles will work for ALL addictions. In this book, I'm going to show you step by step just how I did it, and then you can do it for yourself.

You have to understand just how much God loves you, so that you can learn to love yourself, so that you can learn to love others.

THE C.O.N.N.E.C.T METHOD

The definition of connect is: to join, link, or fasten together; unite or bind.

The more I learn in life, the more I understand just how much I was disconnected from life itself, for too many years. I was searching for love, but in all the wrong places. I thought drugs and alcohol were love because at one time they made my body feel good, but that's just a trap the devil captures you in. When I finally got the addiction chains broken off of me and was free of that delusion, I could see clearly just what love really was and how important it is to stay connected to it. Optimism is a daily spiritual practice, meaning that in order to be happy, you have to put in some work. You have to be connected to an energy source that gives you power every day.

My energy source is God. To me, God is love because God is everything. I believe that when you can go outside and watch the wind blow through the trees and admire the mysterious beauty, that's connection. I believe that when you can see a stranger walking down the same aisle as you at the Wally World and you can speak to them and bring a smile to their face, that's connection. I believe that when you can look yourself in the eyes in your own mirror and smile, knowing that despite all the hurdles you've faced, you gave it your very best, that's connection. I believe that when you learn to love yourself, you can find beauty in everything and everyone, and that's connection.

I believe LOVE is the key to living a happy, vibrant life. You have to understand just how much God loves you, so that you can learn to love yourself, so that you can learn to love others. In order to allow LOVE to flow through you, you have to connect your Mind, Body, and Soul together so that they can operate as one unit, which is the true version of YOU!

I always knew there was a deeper side to me, a side of me that always was curious about things that were never talked about in the environment I came from. That's not to say it was good or bad; it just didn't satisfy my curiosity. I probably could've done more to learn more on my own, but instead of looking like the odd ball, I tried to "fit in" because I wanted love that bad. The only problem with "fitting in" was that I wasn't living the true version of Amanda. And not living as the true Amanda resulted in many years of living a life that was so way off the path that God intended for me.

Once I was ready to throw in the towel on that life forever, God said, "Are you ready for the life I have planned for you?" I had to try, because the life I was living was going nowhere fast. When I put one foot on that right path, my intuition said, "Yep, this is it." I felt a peace, even though I had no clue where my life was heading. I let go of everything I'd ever known. God showed me, little by little, all the work I had to do to C.O.N.N.E.C.T. to his purpose for me and to the true version of myself. I got stretched, I experienced pain, I experienced joy, but ultimately I experienced what LOVE truly is. I'm most grateful for that, since I'd been searching for it for so long.

God said, "First my daughter, I need you to 'Completely live in faith.' That's something you've never ever done before, but it's necessary in order to receive all the blessings I have for you. And just so you know, most people won't understand why you do what you do, but that's ok, because I have big plans for you. I just need you to trust me with everything in you and obey what I tell you to do." I agreed.

God then told me that no one would believe in me or believe that I can make anything of myself, so "Only you need to believe. You will have to learn your worth and understand that I put you here for a reason, Amanda. You will have doubters and you will have people trying to knock you back down, but I need you to expect a new life and expect everything that I have in store for you is amazing."

"'New Clan Time' will be your next order of business. You will have to completely remove yourself from everyone. This will be difficult, but you are so much stronger than you ever can imagine. You have strength through me. You will have to learn what it's like to be alone and learn yourself all over again. When you're done with that task, you will then be able to search out new people, but only those people that make your heart smile, because now you are understanding your worth and you know that a good support system is so important.

"In order to keep your thoughts under control, you will have to 'Nurture that Noggin' every single day and sometimes over and over again, especially on the days when you feel weak. I need you to develop a spirit of gratitude so that you understand just how blessed you are to be alive. Learn to say 'thank you' for the smallest things, because you will appreciate life on such a deeper level. Be mindful of the things you put between your ears, my precious child, because where your focus goes, your energy flows.

"Not only do I want you to feed your mind with goodness, but I want you to 'Energize your vessel' and feed your body with goodness, too. Remember I blessed you with only one for your whole life; I need you to honor me with it and take the upmost care of it. Get your daily exercise in and fuel it with nutrients daily.

"I need you to heighten your awareness of others around you and 'Continuously make a stranger smile' everywhere you go. Sometimes, my child, you will be the only ray of sunshine someone sees and I need you to make a lasting impression so it floods them with hope. I need others to see me through you. I need them to know that something is different about you, so that they want whatever it is you have, which is me.

"Everywhere you go I need you to 'Throw out help,' no matter how big or small the job may seem to you. You will be the missing link for some things to operate smoothly. You will be that person that people can always count on when there is a need to be filled. Help my people with a smile on your face and a song in your heart, because they will be super contagious and spread like wildfire. Remember that you went through certain things because I know I can count on you to show compassion to people on a deep level when they need love the most.

"If you do all these things I ask you to do, my child, this is how you will C.O.N.N.E.C.T. to the amazing woman I intended for you to be. This is how you will C.O.N.N.E.C.T. to the love I've always wanted you to experience."

This is how God showed me to live my life now. The C.O.N.N.E.C.T. Method is my lifestyle.

Completely live in faith

Only you need to believe

New clan time

Nurture that noggin

Energize your vessel

Continuously make a stranger smile

Throw out help

Are you ready to live life like God intends for you to live? He has big plans for you! All you have to do is trust and obey, for there's no other way. I am honored to share with you how I was able to get from being a worthless addict to living a happy, vibrant life. In this book, I break down The C.O.N.N.E.C.T. Method and the baby steps I discovered that changed my life forever. This is no "quick fix" book. This book will teach you a brand new lifestyle that is full of love and joy. I'm looking forward to growing with you! xoxo

The person you were in the past and the things you did back then don't define you now.

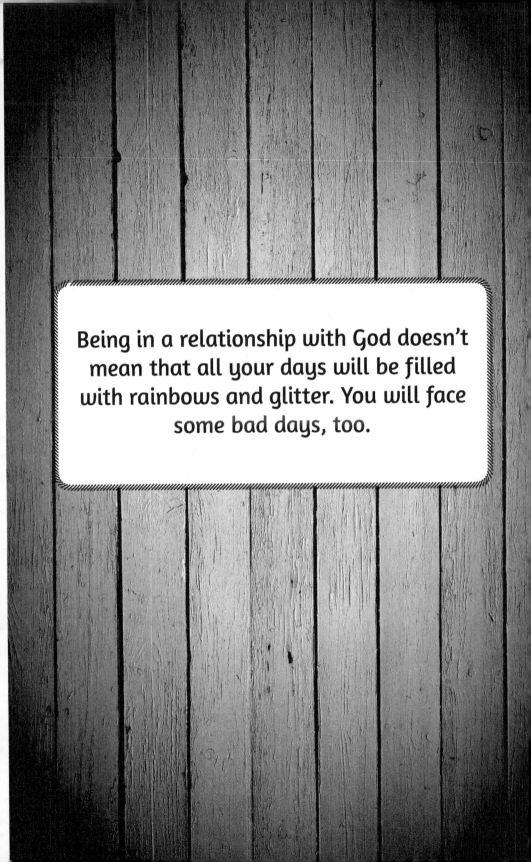

Being in a relationship with God doesn't mean that all your days will be filled with rainbows and glitter. You will face some bad days, too.

COMPLETELY LIVE IN FAITH

Develop a Relationship with God:

God wants to give you all that your heart desires; all you have to do is trust in him.

Honestly, God was the last option for me. I was raised in a Southern Baptist Church and my dad was the Minister of Music for as long as I can remember. For sure, there were good times in the church, but the older I got, I just felt something wasn't right about it. I remember a lot of fussing and fighting over silly stuff, which made me turn my nose up at the whole idea of the God thing. I don't recall being taught how to have a relationship with God, and for whatever reason, I couldn't recall any of the Bible stories I should've been taught in all those years I was in church. I think part of me didn't understand or I couldn't wrap my head around that these stories are real. For so long, they seemed like a fiction book, and were too far-fetched for my brain to understand.

And you know how it is when all the athletes and singers get interviewed and always the first thing out of their mouth is, "I just have to give thanks to God!'"? I always thought they did that to show off. Every single time I heard that, I rolled my eyes. For so long, I didn't even want to hear about God. I couldn't understand why—if God is oh, so great —my life was such a mess. And that's because I didn't have the right perspective nor did I see him as being in control of everything. I never saw any evidence in the people I was going to church with that they had the kind of life I wanted. They all seemed to have just as many problems as I did and complained about all of them, just like I did.

When I was driving from Mississippi to Florida, I turned on praise and worship music, for the first time in a long time. I still wasn't ready to fully surrender, but I asked God to take care of me. I said, "I don't even know if you're real, but please—if you are, keep me safe. I kept seeing clouds shaped like turtles (which symbolized shelter to me), like God was saying, "Don't you worry. You will have a place to stay." And sure enough, it all worked out.

One day, shortly after I'd moved, I went to the beach to clear my head and got a 6-pack of Coors Light on the way. I was super stressed, so the beers were going down real quick and smooth. But the more I drank, the more my heart was hurting. I started crying and said, "I don't know if you're out there, God, but I need a sign that everything is going to be okay." I looked up in the sky for some reason and for a few seconds, in the clouds I saw a muscle flexing, plain as day. To me, God was saying, "You have the strength for this. You already moved to a new state; you can't be scared now." I didn't quit drinking that day, but I couldn't get that cloud out of my head. A couple weeks went by and I saw another muscle flexing in the clouds after another super stressful day. I thought, "There's got to be something to these clouds." These clouds really did something to my soul. I was exhausted from all the years of trying to live life my way. I was exhausted from always trying to fill this emptiness I felt. I really felt God in that moment. I felt this indescribable strength come over me like I could conquer the world. Okay, so maybe not the whole world, but at the least the world I'd been living in. It was time to have dominion over this addiction.

I say August 10, 2015 is my sobriety date, but what it really is, is the day I fully surrendered and let "Jesus take the wheel." I didn't really know how all this worked or what was going to happen, but I knew it had to be a better life than what I'd been living. I said, "God, I'm tired of doing this on my own. Please show me the way." I knew the Bible was an important tool, so I had to dive in. At first, I couldn't comprehend a whole chapter, so I started reading one verse a day and applied it to my life. I promise you, I was super intimidated that I didn't know the stories in the Bible like some folks do, but I don't believe God wants us to memorize the Bible like that. I personally think he's much happier with the application of the verses.

To me, having a relationship with God is putting him first, above everything. It's about asking him for the next right moves and then obeying what he says to do. God wants all his children to be happy and joyful, no matter what you're facing. Being in a relationship with God doesn't mean that all your days will be filled with rainbows and glitter. You will face some bad days, too. A wise man once said to me, "That's like thinking you can live somewhere where there's only sunshine and no bad weather." That's impossible. But what it does mean is that, with God, you will have peace and joy when you face adversity or obstacles. I seriously thought that, when I set out to live a better life, it was going to be easy. Sometimes God allows us to go through some things, because we are lacking something or we need to learn a lesson, but it all works together for our good.

Obedience is the key to living a fulfilling life. For a long time, I couldn't figure out how God was supposed to speak to me, but once I did, my life changed. You know how your gut can tell you if things are right or wrong? Kind of like an internal impression? That's God speaking. He also speaks to me in by sending the same message over and over in different forms. It could be an email, or a billboard, or maybe something I heard on a podcast, but it all carries the same underlying message, so then I start digging a little deeper to figure out what it is I'm supposed to do.

Being in relationship with God is beautiful, and once you realize God isn't out to hurt you and he's here to help you, your life will never be the same. If you're ready to let go of your old ways of doing things, if you're tired and you just can't continue on, if you're ready to succeed in your life, repeat after me...

☆ *Get 'er done:*

> *Dear God, today I choose you. I need you to help me in my life because I can't do this by myself anymore. I'm ready to trust you! Amen.*

Pray Always:

I used to make fun of people that prayed about everything. I heard all the time, "Just pray about it". I always thought, "For what?" I didn't understand the power of prayer until I decided to get in a relationship with God. Prayer is like having a conversation. Prayer is staying constantly connected to the power source.

I have window units for air conditioning in my house. In order for those window units to work properly, they must be plugged into the electrical outlet on the wall. That is their power source. That's where they connect to be able to blow out cold air. If they aren't plugged in, they don't work. It's the same with you. In order to have an amazing relationship with God, you have to stay connected, and the way to stay connected is through prayer.

I pray about everything, ya'll. I am now one of those people that I used to make fun of. And I'm totally okay with it. When things are going great, I pray and give thanks to God. When things are building my character (days of struggle) and I don't feel as if I have any strength to keep going, I pray to God for help. When there are things I want to accomplish and I don't have the funds to make it happen, I pray that God will provide a way.

I used to be shy about praying for the things I truly wanted, but what I've come to realize is that God places the desires in your heart in the first place. You "have not" because you "ask not." Once you've given thanks to God, be real with him and acknowledge your weaknesses. Ask him to help you in the areas you're struggling in. Ask him to help you chase your dreams.

Ask him what the next right move is in your life. But then the key to success is obeying the route he's told you to follow.

I think the hardest part in life is learning to trust him fully and obey what he says. It's not the work itself; that's the easy part. When you pray about something, make sure you're ready to take on the burden of the blessing. No blessing comes with an easy route. No blessing will come without tests along the way. I believe this is so God gets every bit of the glory and you can testify of his goodness to others. You've heard the saying, "Be careful what you wish for." It's the same thing with prayer: "Be careful what you pray for." You can ask God for everything; just make sure you're ready to handle everything that comes with it!

The moment you start seeing God answering your prayers and helping you through tough times and providing ways when there doesn't seem to be any possible way, this strengthens your faith. The stronger your faith gets, the easier it is to face anything head on, because you know that, no matter what you face, God will be right there with you to provide. I don't limit my prayer to once a day. I constantly talk to God throughout my day. I realized just how much I need him and how important it is to stay connected.

The more you grow in Christ, the better you will become at praying. At first, I wasn't sure how to do it and was embarrassed to pray in front of people because everyone else's prayers seemed to be so much deeper than mine. Shoot! I was even embarrassed to pray to God because I didn't want him judging my prayers, either, but I had to get over that real quick. As long as you approach it with a sincere heart, he understands. You have to crawl before you can walk, so you can't expect your prayer life to be like someone else's who has been doing it for 25 years. Start small and grow. The main thing is that you are continually growing. You can start each day with a simple prayer like this until you get comfortable with talking with him deeper...

⭐ Get 'er done:

> Dear God, thank you for waking me up today. Today, please help me be the best version of myself I can be. Amen!

Live in Expectancy

Once you send up a prayer request to God, it's important to act as if it's already come to pass. Thank him in advance for the things you've prayed for. For instance, if you've prayed for a new job, you could say, "God, I'm thanking you in advance for blessing me with this new job. I thank you in advance for allowing me to work in a place where I will be able to use my gifts." It's not that God doesn't want to give you what you've prayed for, but most people don't believe that what they pray for will ever happen, so it never does. It sounds so elementary, but it's so true. If you believe, eventually—in God's time—it will happen.

On my road to being addiction-free, it seemed like life just kept hitting me hard every which way it could. I felt like it was testing me to see just how badly I wanted to live a good life now. The day the apartment manager knocked on my door and told me we had to get out brought me down to my knees in tears. I never in a million years thought I'd have to face another eviction. I'd just experienced an eviction in 2015 from worshipping a drug and alcohol addiction. Now I'm doing my best to live an amazing life and here we are again, in the same predicament, but this time with no car (I'll explain this in another chapter). I really was working hard on building my character back up so people would trust me again, but I'd made some decisions (still based in my addiction mindset) that caused another predicament in my life. I didn't have a job, but I was working hard to build myself up and I just assumed that the bills would get paid. I was starting to "build my brand" and thought the money would just start piling in. Oh, my gosh! That's so far from the truth. I had to be humbled yet again in my life. I never had a problem with living in expectancy, but you also have to put in the work so God can bless you.

Instead of being mad at God, I decided to pray and believe that he had better things in store. I had no idea where we were going to go, but me and my daughter packed a suitcase and headed down the road with our dog. We walked for what seemed to be hours, but it was only a few miles to the nearest hotel. I'd scraped up just enough to stay for a couple of days, but when I got to this particular one, they told me they wouldn't let us stay because they didn't accept dogs. My heart shattered into a million pieces. I couldn't hold the tears in anymore. The whole walk there I'd done my best not to let me daughter see me cry, but I couldn't stop them at this point. I know if I'd had a bad attitude, the whole process would've been so much worse, but I knew God had it all worked out and I believed that no matter what happened, soon enough it would work itself out.

My pride was hurt. I felt like I had let my daughter down AGAIN. It takes a lot to raise a child by yourself, but to only have your child back in your home for less than a year and now we are homeless because I still just couldn't get it together? Man, that was hard. But I sucked it up and swallowed my pride and realized in that moment that I couldn't do any of this by myself. I HAD to reach out for help. I'm a firm believer when you're ready to accept help, God puts the right people in your life that will help you. That was a huge lesson for me to learn. I thought for so long that I could do everything by myself, but I was soon learning that I actually needed people in every aspect of my life. Thankfully, we were able to stay with a friend for a few days until I could get everything sorted out. I am forever grateful for her coming to pick us up and opening her home up to us. Unfortuantely, we couldn't stay there very long, because I had to get closer to my daughter's school.

No mom wants to live with their child in a hotel, but that's what I had to do for a while. I finally found one that would let my dog stay with us, but it smelled like someone has just smoked a whole carton of cigarettes in it right before we got there. I was thankful to just have to a roof over our heads. There were so many people who helped us during this period of time, I can't even properly express the love I felt from everyone that reached out their arms to provide. We had folks sending money to help pay for nights at the hotel so we wouldn't end up on the streets. There were people that paid for food and sent care packages. This is the first time in my life I'd felt loved by so many people and it felt amazing. I'd gotten my car back by this time so I was able to get a job as a server and worked as much as I could to save money to get another place one day. I could've woken up each day, saying, "Why did you do this to me, God?" but instead I woke up each day thanking God in advance for the house he was preparing for me. We often get so consumed with what's not going right that we can't even see past it to find a solution.

I lived in that hotel for two months. The hot water in that place was a hit or miss. There were days I'd get off work and just want to take a hot shower, but only the cold water would work. I had to just be grateful I could take a shower at all. I cried so hard on those nights, because I was exhausted. It wasn't easy some days, but I made it work.

I believed God was going to provide us a house before my daughter started school, so we could have a permanent address. On August 2nd, we moved in to our very own house. She started school on August 10th. Because I expected God to provide a way and I believed it would happen, it did! I never gave up on the days when I couldn't see anything happening. I never gave up on the days when I felt like I couldn't go any further.

Do you know that, when I was looking around for houses and apartments, the only one I got to see inside of is the one I live in now? How crazy is that? When I got to look inside this house, I knew I didn't have any furniture to fill it up with, but I still envisioned some being in there. I envisioned where I would put the beds and the couch. When I moved in, I literally had an air mattress and a few dishes. Now I have a fully-furnished house, because I saw it as if it had furniture in it and thanked God in advance for it all.

Lil Babies, this kind of living sometimes doesn't come naturally for some, but I promise you that—with work—you too can build up this muscle and live in expectancy with all aspects of your life. You WILL come up against adversity and struggle; of that there is no doubt. It's called life. But whatever you face, you HAVE to know that it's already worked out. You HAVE to believe that it's only temporary. You HAVE to live in the future to a certain degree and act "as if."

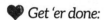 *Get 'er done:*

Repeat after me...

Even though I'm currently facing _____, I KNOW good things are on the way and I am determined not to give up.

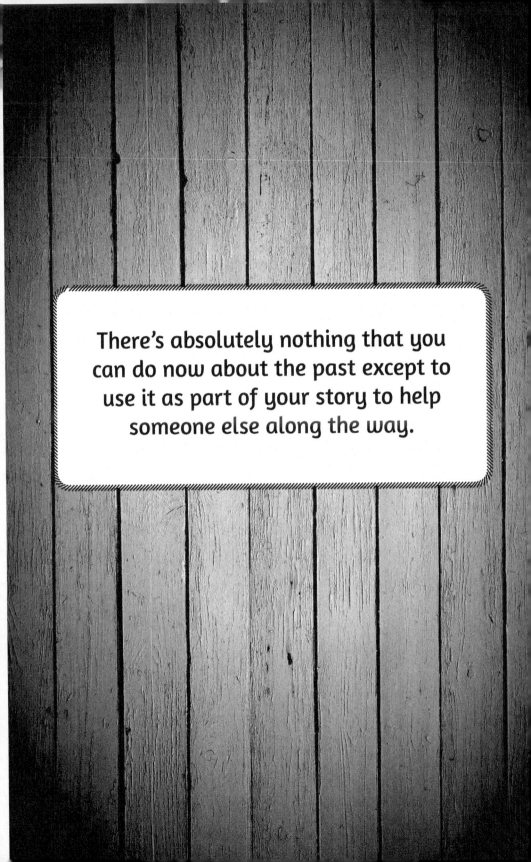

There's absolutely nothing that you can do now about the past except to use it as part of your story to help someone else along the way.

ONLY YOU NEED TO BELIEVE

Forgive Yourself

For so long, folks called me worthless. They said I would never amount to anything. I know you've heard similar things over and over again, too. When you hear all these negative things about yourself all the time, you start believing it. In our addiction, we make bad decisions, but that doesn't mean that we are bad people. If you're anything like me, you've damaged many relationships over the years, so you don't have a cheering squad to encourage your new journey. That's okay, because a cheering squad isn't going to help if *you* don't believe in yourself. How can I believe in someone that I don't even love? That's the question I kept replaying over and over again in my head. I believe that in order for us to *love* ourselves we must first *forgive* ourselves.

I'm sure you've already heard of making amends with people. I firmly believe in that when the time is right, but you can't make amends with someone if you haven't even come to terms with the situation yourself. As I said, my last arrest was a felony. I was so caught up in my addiction, I felt entitled to steal checks from my employer and make them payable to myself. I had no awareness of what those actions would do to his family. I didn't love myself, so how could I possibly love or care about anyone else? My point is that, until I forgave myself for the damage I'd done, it did absolutely no good to reach out and apologize to him, because it wouldn't have been sincere.

What I came to terms with is that there's no way I can go back and change my actions; what's done is done. And though it was so out of keeping with my true character, I had to take full ownership for those actions: "Yep, I did that. I actually stole from someone." Just through the act of admitting it out loud to myself, I could feel a huge weight lifted off my shoulders. A lot of my problem for so many years was that I blamed everyone else for my actions, but the minute I took responsibility for them, my life started changing and I could see myself as a different person.

I will be growing and learning until the day I die, but I can say I am a better person today than I was yesterday. It took over a year before I was ready to write my old employer an apology. To this day, I don't know if he got it or read it, but I do know that—in the moment I wrote it—I was sincere because I had forgiven myself. When you get into a relationship with God, did you know he forgives you for everything you've done? Did you know he wipes your slate clean each day? So, if God loves us and forgives us, why is it so hard to love and forgive ourselves? I know that in my life, it was because I felt as if I could never measure up because of all my failures.

First, I need you to only control what you *can* control and not worry about the rest. You can't control what others think of you, so I need you to stop paying attention to it. Next get out a few pieces of paper and a marker (preferably a bright-colored one). Write in big letters "I'm AMAZING!" "I'm BEAUTIFUL/HANDSOME" "I'm a WINNER" "I'm a SURVIVOR" "I can do ALL things through Christ, who gives me strength." Fill these pieces of paper with positive affirmations about yourself and tape them on your mirror, your walls, your desk—anywhere that you will see them every single day. Even if you don't believe them at first, please do yourself a favor and just do it anyways. Part of learning to love yourself is believing that you are worthy of happiness!

We have to flood our mind with these positive vibes so we can wash out all the negative things people have ever said. The battle we face each day is in our own mind, not out there somewhere. When you start replacing all the negative thoughts in your mind with encouraging ones, you can then understand that the person you were in the past and the things you did back then don't define you now. There's absolutely nothing that you can do now about the past except to use it as part of your story to help someone else along the way. There's no use in holding onto unnecessary baggage when you've already been forgiven by the one and only Creator. The more you see these affirmations, the sooner you will start believing them! So, stop what you're doing right now and let's get them up!

When we ask God's forgiveness for our sins, I think the devil does his best to keep that hold on us. Today is the day you are going to fully surrender that thing that has been weighing you down. You have been carrying it around for far too long. It's time to get your life back.

♥ *Get 'er done:*

Repeat after me:

Today I'm letting go of _____ forever. I am tired of you having control over my life. You will no longer keep me from being the amazing person I was born to be.

Mirror Talkin'

Now that you've gotten your positive affirmations where you can see them every single day, I need you to start speaking life into yourself when you get in front of the mirror. I want you to look yourself in the eyes and tell yourself the things that you have written down. It was so hard for me to look myself in the eyes and say things like, "I'm amazing and I deserve to be happy." I didn't believe it at first. It took many, many mirror pep talks before I actually started believing the things I was saying. The first few times I said it, I said it about 10 times in a row and then I started sobbing. It was so hard for me to look myself in the eyes after all the things I'd done and all the people I've hurt. But I kept at it, because no one else believed in me. I had to learn to believe in myself. Every day, no matter how much it hurt, I did this over and over and over. I would say things like "You can do this, Amanda!" "I deserve the best and I accept the best," and all the things I'd taped on my wall. Eventually I started believing the things that were coming out of my mouth. Eventually, I could stand to look at the woman I was seeing in the mirror. Eventually there were no more tears when I gave myself pep talks.

Let me suggest you do this exercise in private at first, because not everyone gets the importance of speaking life into yourself. Once you start believing and get comfortable with the words you are saying to yourself, then by all means let the world know. I just want you to believe in yourself FIRST! Every morning when I take my daughter to school, she does the same mirror pep talks. I never had anyone speak life into me growing up, much less did I speak life into myself. I know this boosts her confidence. I know that as she grows into being a woman, she will know the importance of believing in herself and, more importantly, she will always have someone believe in her.

Lil Babies, if my high-schooler can do this every day, I know you can do it, too! I truly believe that everyone on this earth deserves the opportunity to be happy, no matter what they may have done. Grab your mirrors and start right now. Don't waste any more time thinking of yourself as a loser! I believe in you, and it's time you start believing in you, too.

Remember I didn't have that cheering squad for quite a while. I had burned so many bridges, no one believed a word out of my mouth anymore. That's a hard pill to swallow, but it was reality. I HAD to make sure I was there for myself. I HAD to make sure that I did the necessary work to show them that I was serious. Everyone's heard the famous line, "Actions speak louder than words." So, if I already know that people aren't going to believe in me, I have to learn how to believe in myself because no one else wants to even be around me. So, if you're serious about changing, you have to do things you've never EVER done before. It may feel silly, but it's so very important.

Forgiving yourself and loving yourself are probably the simplest (but also the hardest) things for us to do. We get too consumed with comparing our lives to others. I did this A LOT at first. "If I hadn't wasted all those years in my addiction, I could've had this, like so and so." What you have to realize is that no one else's life is like yours. No one else can ever get the blessings that you were intended to get. And vice versa. Comparing your life to someone else's is such a dangerous way to live.

Understand that you went through all the things you went thru for a specific reason. Being proud of your mistakes and owning up to your mistakes are two completely different things. You don't necessarily need to "happy dance" because of the things you did; you just have to admit to them and forgive yourself for them. You DO need to be proud of yourself for taking the first step toward living the best life possible. Be proud of yourself because you have done some amazing things in life. Trust me, there are days I feel weak. Those are the days I make sure I speak life into myself as much as I can. Every time I see a mirror, I give myself a pep talk, even if I don't believe those words at that moment. There's power in repeating it to yourself over and over and over.

 Get 'er done:

> *Stop what you're doing right now and get to a mirror. Repeat after me....*

> *"I'm AMAZING!!" "I deserve to be happy!" "I am worthy of a happy life!" "I deserve the best and I accept the best!"*

I learned that other people's opinions of me didn't make them my reality.

You can't expect to live a different life if you aren't willing to change the people you hang around.

The good thing about getting a new clan is they don't know your past unless you tell them.

NEW CLAN TIME

Distance Yourself from Your Old Clan

Lil Babies, I know this is a difficult thing to do, but I promise that you will thank me later. Think of the top 5 people you hang around with right now. Do they add value to your life or do they suck energy from your life? Are they living a happy, sober life, or are they still using and running the streets? You can't expect to live a different life if you aren't willing to change the people you hang around. Trust me when I tell you this. I've tried so many times to live a better life but would still hang out with the same old people. It's not that they were bad people by any means; they just didn't have the same intentions as I did.

When I first moved down to Florida, I instantly attracted the same type of people that had been in my life in Mississippi, because really that's all I'd known for so many years—the party people. They were living life the same way I had lived for so long, just in a different state. A wise man once said to me, "You don't know what you don't know." If all you know is a certain type of people, you really have no idea what else is out there in the world if you don't break away from them. You can't possibly know what else is out there in the world if you don't get out of your comfort zone—the one that you've been living in for so many years.

The last time I ever hung out with "the party people" was the last time I put any drugs or alcohol in my body. I met up with some folks for a friend's birthday at a bar in the next city over from me. I'd known some of these people for many, many years, because I'd lived in Florida previously The problem was that they were still living the same way they had been living when I left them, with no signs of wanting a better life. The drinks were going down super fast and super smooth. I remember playing darts and then the next memory I had was of standing on the sidewalk, downtown all alone, back in the city where I lived. I had no idea how I got there or where I was exactly, and for the first time in a long time, I was scared to death. Something seriously bad could've happened to me. It was weird to me because, in all those years I'd been in my addiction, I never cared about the "what ifs," but they started flooding into my mind, like "what if I'd gotten hit by a car," "what if I ended up at someone's house I didn't know and they raped me," "what if I got robbed while standing on the street corner and someone stabbed me." I started to almost have an anxiety attack, but I had to get myself together and concentrate on how to get home.

My daughter immediately flashed in my vision. I started crying that hard, sloppy cry. I knew at that drunken moment, I couldn't do this anymore. I couldn't hang out with people that did the very things that had destroyed my life for so many years. I'm not saying they're bad people; they're not that at all. I'm not judging them or how they choose to live their life, but I am saying that if I wanted to change my life, I HAD to let them go. I did want to change. That's why I had packed up and moved in the first place. I didn't come all this way just to continue the life I was living. Let's face it: I was going to end up in jail for a long time or dead if something didn't change soon, and neither one of those were an attractive option for me.

I was scared of being alone; I was scared of making new friends, but I knew it was necessary. I knew it was time to step out of my own comfort zone some more. To this day, I haven't seen any of that crew, not because I think I'm better than them, but because I love myself enough to put myself around people that bring out the best in me. Folks may get upset when you choose to live a better life or they may not even care at all, which can sometimes hurt a little worse. If either of these happen, you know you made the right choice. People that genuinely care about you will always respect your decisions and most definitely want to see you live a happy life. There are so many people in this world to choose from as the ones you want to be in your life. When you do your mirror talkin' each day, remember just how important you are and that you deserve the best.

> **Folks may get upset when you choose to live a better life or they may not even care at all, which can sometimes hurt a little worse. If either of these happen, you know you made the right choice.**

I am here to testify that as uncomfortable as it may be at first and as scary as it may be, you will start to notice some big changes in your life as soon as you remove yourself from people that don't have your best interests at heart. To this day, I still sit and think about all the different kinds of people I once hung out with. I've seen people shoot up meth in their veins. I've been around thieves. I've been around folks that had no ambition whatsoever. It makes me sad that I was labeled as being those things just because I hung around them, whether I was partaking in the activity or not. Guilty by association. You are going to be like the people you hang out with the most. So, unless you want to be labeled with those things for the rest of your life (and I know you don't, because deep down you know you deserve more), please do yourself a favor and for 30 days love yourself enough to remove those labels people place on you by who you hang out with. If you don't see your life dramatically change in those 30 days, feel free to go back to your old ways. But I know without a doubt that, once you start seeing the change, you won't have the desire to go back.

⭐ Get 'er done:

> Make a list of the 5 people you hang out with the most. Write the pros and cons to hanging out with these people. Do they encourage you daily or are they dragging you down? If they drag you down, for 30 days gradually distance yourself from them. I'm not saying you have to completely give up that relationship; just distance yourself from them so you can grow.

Be Your Own Clan for a While

I used to hate even the thought of being by myself for any length of time. I don't know why we (as humans) are so scared of learning about our true self. It's quite an amazing experience— discovering your strengths and weaknesses, too! In between me letting go of the old friends and bringing in the new ones, I really didn't even have a choice except to spend time alone with myself, since had I decided to let go of the only people I really knew in Florida. I was always the girl that had folks over at my house all the time or I was always at someone else's house. Being alone with all the thoughts in their head is enough to make anyone sick to their stomach at first, but it's just like anything else: once you do it and keep doing it, it does get easier and better.

I had no idea what to do with myself, so here's where I started. In the next chapter, I will talk about the importance of daily motivation, but one of the many things I learned was to write down things. I write down everything. I heard the question somewhere, "If money wasn't an issue, where would you be and/or what would you be doing?" My first thought was, "This is dumb. I don't have any money, so it doesn't really matter." But that question kept replaying in my head and I was intrigued. I played along, but only because it was bugging the heck out of me. (Haha) So I grabbed a notebook and wrote down a couple things (create a redneck workout, own a beach house, own a black Chevy Silverado, etc.). The more I thought about the things that I wrote down, the more I realized that I could make them happen. I wasn't really sure how, but just the thought of it made me excited. Before I knew it, a couple hours had gone by, just by me thinking and writing. Oh, my gosh. I did it! I spent time by myself and it was actually kind of cool.

I can't remember exactly how far into my new life this got easier, but it wasn't an overnight fix. It was a process and I had to learn to be patient with myself through it all. I cried, I laughed, I happy-danced, I got frustrated—so many different emotions and, honestly, I still do those same things today. Though I'm completely comfortable with being by myself these days, actually it's much-needed time in this crazy world that we live in. It's a way I can get back to my center and get my mind back in the right place. It's a way to write down all my goals and dreams and no one will ever laugh at me. It's really a beautiful process. Sometimes I just sit and think about where I once was and how much I've grown as a person. It makes me smile. I'm so freakin' proud of myself! There's no way I could've ever said those words to myself if I hadn't learned all about me, all over again. You will get there. Start with baby steps.

⏰ *Get 'er done:*

> *For 30 days straight, spend at least 30 minutes by yourself. Turn the TV off. Turn the phone off. Tune the world out. Think about some of the things you would do if money wasn't an issue. Think about some amazing memories. Write them down. The more you do this, the more you will learn about yourself. And the more you learn about yourself, the more you learn to love and value yourself.*

Google Folks You Would Like to Hang With

Technology is so powerful. Y'all know you can get on that internet thing and type whatever you want and have immediate results, right? Alright, so once I separated from my old clan and learned how to spend time with myself, I was now ready to search for people I wanted to hang out with. I grabbed my handy dandy notebook and made a list of the things I always wanted to do and that I loved to do. I had to do some serious thinking because, over the 17 years I was lost in addiction, I'd totally lost myself, too. Of all the things I could think of in the whole world, I remembered there was a time I had wanted to do a Mud Run. I'd seen some ads on Facebook years before and all I could think about was how much fun that would be. But when I was lost in my addiction, I didn't have anyone that would do one with me and at that time, I was too scared to let go of the people I had in my inner circle, so I never went. But spending time alone, that memory popped up in my mind out of the blue.

It's really amazing what you come up with when you quiet the world around you and just think. So I Googled just that... "Mud Runs Tampa Bay." I wish I had a more brilliant plan of attack to give you, but it's literally that simple. I'm not going to lie, this was nerve-wracking for me. It's a super easy step to take, or at least it sounds like it, but I didn't know if these people would accept me. I still wasn't completely confident with the girl I saw in the mirror. I definitely had grown some by this time, but I still didn't have anyone from my past that give me that gold star approval. I was still pretty much my own cheering squad.

My palms were sweating and my heart was racing but I took a deep breath and sent an email to one of the contacts I found. I waited nervously for an email to come back and it did! It turns out I had reached out to some pretty welcoming people that invited me to attend a fitness class and train with them. Can you imagine the smile on my face? I'm smiling just thinking about it, because not only did I overcome a fear of rejection, but I also stepped out of my comfort zone and made some new friends. About a month or so of going to this new fitness class and training, I got my very own medal at an Obstacle Course Race (Mud Run).

I did it!!! I accomplished something I always wanted to and I did it SOBER and with a new clan. The good thing about getting a new clan is they don't know your past unless you tell them. They don't judge you for what you used to be, because they didn't know you then. It's a win-win situation! I ended up doing several Obstacle Course Races with these fine folks and had such an amazing time at each one of them. Some of them are still in my life to this day.

Going to hang out with new people can be a little overwhelming and weird at first, but remember: you have to get out of your comfort zone if you seriously want things to change in your life. So, you've distanced yourself from the old clan. You've hung out by yourself, learning to love the person you see in the mirror. Now you have to allow others to love you. You really only have two options: you can either keep the same old crowd and do the same old things, or you can be a little uncomfortable for a short period of time and create some lifelong relationships. The beautiful thing is that everyone is seeking that love and acceptance, so those people you are looking to meet, they are also searching for the same thing. There's really no need to even be nervous, but (for some reason) we as humans always have that fear of rejection. It's so silly, if you really think about it, especially since everyone is ultimately searching for the same thing.

Most cities these days have lots and lots of different meetups with lots of different people from lots of different walks of life. There's no excuse for you not to find your new clan. There are some amazing people out there, just waiting for you to join their group. It's not going to be complete until you get there, so whatcha waiting on? Get to Googling.

☆ *Get 'er done:*

Get a piece of paper and list 5 things that you love to do or always wanted to do. Now get on your computer and Google people that do those things in your city or a nearby city. Find some contact information and reach out to them. Once you find out when y'all can meet up, GO!!!! Take some deep breaths before you go and enjoy yourself. You got this!!!!!!!!

If you take something away, you HAVE to replace it with something else!

NURTURE THAT NOGGIN

Daily Motivation

How intentional have you been about what you feed your mind? Have you ever paid attention before? I sure didn't, until I decided to change my life. In order to change though, I had to do things I'd never done before. I got introduced to personal development and I promise you, at first I had no idea what the heck it was. I started by listening to YouTube videos of people talking all positive and using language I'd never heard before. The very first one I listened to was a mix of several guys, but there was something about what they said hit me hard in my heart. It was as if they were talking directly to me. As soon as it was over, I felt like I could conquer the world. I felt empowered! I'd never heard of a motivational speaker in my life, probably because I was too consumed with my addiction to pay attention to anything else, but I craved more.

For the first time in 17 years, I felt like these dudes knew what I was going through. I felt connected to someone that understood me even though they were just on a video. I felt like they had the right answers, so every day I made this a part of my routine. Before I even got out of bed, I made sure to listen to a video. The more I listened, the better I felt. Some days, I listened to the same video, over and over and over and over again. I made it my theme for the day. I learned that I could be anyone I wanted to be! I learned that my past doesn't define me. I learned that other people's opinions of me didn't make them my reality.

I learned that my daughter is my "WHY." She's the reason I decided to change my life in the first place. Do you know what your "WHY" is? What or who is it that makes you get up another day and take a breath, even on the days you want to quit? Is it your mom? Is it your child? It has to be someone or something that gives you that driving force, because those days will come when you feel like giving up. Those days will come when you get frustrated and your "WHY" will be the only thing that keeps you going.

Whatever you are putting into your mind is going to be the very thing you think about, whether you mean to or not. What kind of music are you listening to? Are you listening to rap that degrades women and talks about smoking weed? Or are you listening to soothing music that uplifts your spirit? Most people don't even realize how much those words have an effect on you. Think about it: If you are listening to music about smoking weed over and over and over because you love the song so much, subconsciously you are thinking about smoking weed all the time. I'm no scientist, so I can't explain how it all works on that kind of level, but I do know that's a true statement. If you are listening to music that has kindness in it, you will automatically want to be kind to someone. It's just the way it works.

I eventually found a new clan that pours daily motivation in me. These are the kind of people you want in your life. You have hit the jackpot when you find people who support you, love you, and uplift you. Daily motivation can also be found in books. Just like you searching for people that do the things you want to do, start reading books about the things you love. I had never read a whole book in my life. I doubted that I could even finish a book, but I finished several that first year. And I actually enjoy it now, because I learn so much from the books I choose to read. Gaining knowledge is exciting to me and I promise you, I wasn't voted most likely to succeed! In high school, I almost didn't graduate because of some papers I was supposed to write on some books I was supposed to read but hadn't.

Coming out of a life that's filled with negativity, that's filled with judgment, that's filled with shame—it's so important to replace all those negative thoughts that once filled your mind with new positive, empowering goodness. If you take something away, you HAVE to replace it with something else. You may be like I was and not have a lot of money to be spending on books and other things. The good news is you can find countless videos on YouTube for free! Just search motivational videos. Also, now there's so many books on YouTube that you can listen to, so there's no excuse as to why you can't start this activity today.

Feeding your mind is just as important as feeding your body with good food. If you put junk in, expect to feel like crap and only put junk back out into the world. But if you feed your mind with goodness, you can expect to put goodness back into the world. This is necessary in becoming the best version of you. I know you have so much potential you haven't even begun to experience all you can offer. It will blow your mind once you become consistent with personal development. Remember, you were created for a specific reason! You have a purpose on this earth and if you want to experience all that God has for you, you must take these small action steps each day. Don't waste any more of your life away; you've already done enough of that.

⏰ *Get 'er done:*

> *Start small... watch one video each day and read a book for 10 minutes a day, for a week straight. You will begin to see a change happening.*

Trade TV Time

Most of us were raised watching TV, with the thought that that's all there is to do. When you've had a long day at work, plop on the couch and watch TV. When you're hanging out with a significant other, pile up on the couch, snuggle, and watch TV. When you're a kid, watch cartoons on Saturday mornings on TV. When you're trying to go to sleep, turn the TV on. I fell into all of these categories at one point or another, but when I started putting goodness into my mind by way of personal development, I noticed that every time I watched TV it had me feeling a certain way. I'd get stuck on watching *Forensic Files* or *Dateline*, which is all about murders, and that quickly got my mind in a negative space. I always fell asleep with the TV on, and for some reason I woke up irritable every morning. How can you *not* be, when you have nothing but negative vibes blaring all night for your mind to soak up? This is going to sound crazy: I used to love watching *Lifetime* movies, but each time I found myself actually putting myself in the characters' shoes and felt as if I was really going through the same things as they were in the movie. Most those *Lifetime* movies have a lot of drama, so that definitely was a lot of unnecessary drama in my life. Don't play around like you've never done that. I know I'm not the only one!

Since I was changing everything else, one night I decided to try something new and play positive motivation while I went to sleep instead of the TV, and when I woke up the next morning, I could tell a huge difference in my mood. I was actually excited to wake up and start the day instead of waking up with a chip on my shoulder, so I kept doing it every night. I found some free videos on YouTube that were about an hour long so it would shut off at the end of the video. After a couple of weeks, though, I got lazy and decided to go back to my old ways of having the TV on, and just like before, I woke up super irritable again. At that moment, I became a firm believer that what they were telling me on those videos was true. Be cautious about what you allow between your ears! Value yourself enough guard your mind with everything you have, because (remember I told you) that's ultimately where the biggest battle is—in our minds.

I never slept with the TV on again. In fact, I decided to cut it totally out of my life. I'm not suggesting you have to do that completely, but I am suggesting that you cut the time you spend watching it and start thinking about the goals and dreams you wish to accomplish. Did you know that EVERYONE is born with a purpose? Yes, everyone! I used to think that only certain people were born to be "special" in this world and the rest of us were just plain Jane average folks. When I was growing up, no one ever told me that I was born with certain gifts and I was to use them for a specific task! The more personal development I did, the more I learned about this. And the more I learned about this, the hungrier I got for this knowledge. So especially now, there was no need for TV. In my quiet time alone, I started reading books and gathering information everywhere I could. I learned that I have the gifts of Faith and Mercy. I'm still soaking it all in and learning as I go. Can you see how all of this is starting to tie together? You can replace the time you spent watching TV with some of that alone time I asked you to do in the previous chapter. You can then use your alone time to watch those motivational videos or read that book. This is how you start to grow.

Once your eyes are opened to this new life that you're creating, YOU will be hungrier than ever to learn as much as you can about yourself. Remember, I said if you remove something you must replace it, so with you removing some of your TV time, now you have more time for positivity in your life. Just make sure you are replacing the TV time with the right things.

🕐 *Get 'er done:*

Try starting small and giving up 30 minutes each day of the TV time and devote it to researching what gifts you were born with and how YOU could use your gifts to change someone's life. You have that power! You were born to do amazing things. Once you get the 30 minutes down pat, then go up to an hour a day. Before long, you may be like me and not ever have the desire to watch TV, because your desire to help folks became so much greater!

"I'm Grateful for" List

Life served me some hard hits to the gut during my first year of sobriety. I was under the impression that my life would be easy, now that I had chosen to be a better person. That's just not the case. I think life will keep giving you tests, just to see how bad you want it. I experienced my first-ever car repossession. I'd started building my brand, Patched Wangs, but because I was brand new at it all, I seriously thought that it would be an instant money-maker. And by "building my brand," I mean get my message of hope out into the world. God showed me that my business (Patched Wangs) would be coaching and teaching folks how to go from being a broken soul to living a happy life. Although he didn't show me any specific details on how it all would work at the time, or a specific date I was going to start making money by doing this, I had total faith that it was going to work. The sad news is it didn't bring in a dime at first.

I honestly had no idea that building a business and putting your message out into the world takes a couple years to get off the ground good. I know deep down that all great things take time, but our society is based so much on instant gratification, I expected it to boom in the first few weeks. Reality smacked me upside the gourd! I'm definitely a risk-taker, and I will put my whole heart and soul into something if I believe in it, but there was a big problem: I couldn't pay my bills and all the creditors were calling. I know I'd rather be a risk-taker than not, but it doesn't always work out like I envision it; however, there is always a lesson to be learned. So I tried to hold them off as long as I could, but there came a point where I was avoiding their calls. I was ashamed to even tell them that I couldn't pay my bills.

When I heard a knock at the door, I already knew deep down what it was about. Tears just started streaming down my face. I opened the door and there were two men standing there. I could tell he wasn't excited about telling me I had to come outside and get all my belongings out of the car. I can imagine being a repo man is a tough job. . I told him just to take it all; I didn't want anything out of it. It's not that I didn't want it; I seriously didn't want to go through that experience of embarrassment. He insisted I get it cleaned out, so me and my daughter grabbed some trash bags and headed outside to clean it out. I felt like I was going to throw up right there, on the spot. Cleaning out my only means of transportation (with my *daughter*, on top of it all) made me feel like such a failure. Every time I reached inside that car to get my belongings to put in the trash bag, my heart felt like it broke a little bit more. I couldn't even make my eyes watch the tow truck pulling my car away. This was the very first time I'd gotten my car repossessed. I know that I wasn't the only one that has ever experienced this, but in that moment, I felt like my world was crashing down around me. I even thought that maybe I'd made a mistake when I moved to Florida.

How could I look in my daughter's eyes? That's the thing that hurt me the most. It hadn't even been a year yet since she'd moved back in with me. I was trying so hard to rebuild a good life for us and it just seemed like the harder I tried, the more I failed. How was I going to get around town? How was I going to get food for us? All these thoughts were racing around in my head.

That night, sitting on my bed, I tried real hard to be tough for my kiddo, but I just couldn't hold it together. After she came and gave me a big hug and told me "Everything is going to be okay," I knew at that moment I had two choices. I could let this defeat me or I had to find a way to keep pressing on. Instead of focusing on what I *didn't* have, I started thinking about the things I *did* have. I had a roof over my head, clothes to wear, food to eat, a daughter that loves me and depends on me... and suddenly the pain of my car being taken away didn't seem to hurt so bad. Just because I didn't have a car didn't mean my life had stopped. It just meant that I was going to have to try harder to make this work.

The next morning, my daughter got on the bus to go to school and I packed my backpack with my computer and walked 2 miles to Starbucks to use their wifi. Instead of complaining about it, I started saying, "I'm grateful for the ability to even walk, I'm grateful for the desire to keep going, I'm grateful for the shoes on my feet." It really put things in perspective for me. I walked back and forth 4 miles every day so I could continue to build my brand. On my walks, I started noticing all the amazing flowers around me. I literally would stop and smell the flowers. It was something I never would've done in my car. I started finding beauty in nature. The things I normally would've taken for granted (or not even paid attention to) were the very things that were giving me a new perspective on life.

I'm a firm believer that when you can appreciate what you have at the moment, you will be blessed with more. After a week or so of walking, I got blessed with a bike. It was no fancy thing; it was an old beach-cruiser type bike, but man! I was so grateful for it. It had a bar on the back, so my daughter could ride on it, too. We would rig it up with towels so she had a cushion. We made the best of what we had. It also had a basket on the front, so when we needed groceries, I rode the bike to the grocery store.

The first time I did that, I over-calculated how many groceries I could carry on the bike. Needless to say, that bike ride home was a struggle. I had groceries flip-floppin' everywhere. The bags were starting to tear, and I was praying so hard, "Lord, please let me make it home with these bags in one piece." And do you know? No one even stopped to ask if I needed help. The only person that spoke to me was a homeless man, because he understood exactly what I was going through. No one in their cars even bothered to notice me. It really made me sad. We as humans get so caught up in our own lives, we fail to acknowledge others. I promised God that day that if he allowed me to get my car back, I would also make sure to help others that needed a ride. Oh, I did end up getting my car back on the same day I got evicted, so at least if I needed to, I could sleep in it.

You're going to face obstacles in life; you're going to have days where you feel like throwing your hands up in the air and quitting, but on those days, it's most important to put things in the right perspective and list out the things that are going right in your life and the blessings you already have. Simple things, like being thankful for hot water or sheets on your bed, can really change your whole attitude about things. I suggest that, before you even get to the super tough days, start your day off listing out a couple things you're grateful for. That way you're more prepared and it's easier to get your mind back right and get your peace back. Humble yourself before life humbles you!

♥ *Get 'er done:*

Each day before you step out into the world, list 5 things you are grateful for.

You don't have to change everything
all at once.

ENERGIZE YOUR VESSEL

Break a Sweat

Fitness is a MUST to live a life of happiness. Personally, I don't love the whole process of working out, but I do it anyways because I don't like the outcome of living my old life. Something about releasing all the endorphins and dopamine in your brain... Well, I'm not even going to pretend like I know what all that does. All I know is that when I work out, it makes me feel amazing. Remember, when you take something away, you must replace it with something else, so we are all about creating good habits. I spent a lot of time curling beer cans in my day, but now I just curl sweet potatoes. No, seriously. I have to make the workouts fun, so I came up with a Redneck Workout Series. You can literally work out with any object in your house.

The Redneck Workouts aren't about losing weight, or gaining muscle, per se. It's about learning to connect the mind, body, and soul together to live a healthy, vibrant life. You don't have to go out and buy any equipment. You already have all the materials you need. I show you how to build a jug bar with an old broom handle, some milk jugs, and duct tape. You can use this thing for many different exercises. I show you how to build your own homemade weights using Walmart sacks and bottles of water.

All my videos can be found on my website (www.patchedwangs.com) or my YouTube Channel: Patched Wangs. They are designed to bring joy back into your life and offer a baby step to your new life of fitness. Mostly it makes me laugh, which is a good ab workout, so boom! It's a win-win! People sometimes turn their nose up at fitness, because of ideas in their head that it can't be fun. Let me tell you something, people: it can be as fun or as boring as you make it. It has to become a part of your life, just like getting dressed and going to work. Here's another area where trading some TV time can do a body good!

There's so many different ways you can get your fitness in these days. I truly believe this is a missing link in a lot of recovery programs out there. Yes, we most definitely have work to do on our mind and soul, but our body is a temple and we should take care of it. Imagine your dream car for a second. If you had that shiny car in your driveway, wouldn't you take the best care of it you possibly can? Wouldn't you make sure it didn't get a single scratch or dent in it? Wouldn't you keep the interior immaculate? Think of your body this way. I know you would get the oil changed regularly and make sure the gas you put in it was good gas. YOUR BODY IS THE SAME WAY. God blessed you with only one of them, for your whole life.

We take our body for granted so often. We just expect it to be around forever and we expect it to stay healthy. When we haven't been taking good care of it and we get sick or get a disease because of a life of abuse, we throw our hands up in the air and say, "WHY ME?" WHY?? Because you didn't choose to take care of it all those years. Because you decided that you could fill it with junk and it would still function properly. What would happen if you put sugar in the gas tank of your car? It wouldn't run. DUH. A car is made to put only gas in it. A car is made to go, not sit still; it's the same way with you. You have to start moving around, you have to start putting goodness in it, and you have to get plenty of rest so you can function properly. I want you to invite me to your 80ᵗʰ birthday party, so please do yourself a favor and take the necessary steps so that can happen.

I'm talking about "Let's start with baby steps, Lil Babies." Take small, little action steps each day, to start building your new life foundation.

☆ *Get 'er done:*

> *Go join your local gym, go get you a bike, go to yoga class, go to crossfit, do a redneck workout… it doesn't really matter to me what you choose to do. Just do yourself a favor and add a little something to your daily routine. A little sweat does the body good.*

Fill Your Belly with Goodness

It took me a while, but I finally understand what filling your body will goodness really does. One day a light bulb went off inside my brain after I ate a whole box of cookies. The cookies were oh, so good going down, but it really got me in a bad space in my head, my body felt like crap, and it affected my mood. I

realized in that moment how everything is linked together...
Mind, Body, and Soul. Because I overdid it with the cookies and
my stomach was hurting, in my mind, I immediately felt like a
big failure, and because I felt like a failure I didn't have a positive
attitude. It's so super important to keep feeding all three (Mind,
Body, and Soul) with nothing but goodness at all times to make
sure they (all three) stay in tune with each other. Folks get all
weird about changing their foods for some reason, too. You don't
have to change everything all at once. I used to drink about 3
Cokes a day, but I gave that up, too, on the day I decided to get
sober.

Here's how I did it. Each day I made small goals for myself, so
they were easily obtainable. Today I will trade my Coke for
water. Just that simple. I didn't say, "Well, I'm going to TRY to
drink water instead of Coke." Nope. I said, "I WILL trade my Coke
for water." Plain and simple. If you drink a lot of Cokes or sugary
drinks a day, you may have to reduce it slowly with water. Say, if
you drink 3 a day, trade one of those Cokes for water and drink 2
Cokes a day for a week. Then, the next week drink 1 Coke a day
and trade 2 Cokes for water. Then the week after that, you will
be totally on water! I took the same concept with fried foods and
junk food. I traded a little bit at a time with healthy foods (fruits,
veggies, salads, baked foods) until I'm at the point now that if
I eat fried foods, it hurts my stomach, so I just stay away from
them. I promise you, if I eat one little itty bitty French Fry now,
I get so sick! It's crazy, but my body is now so used to ingesting
goodness in, it rejects all the junk.

Don't get overwhelmed with this process and think everything
has to change all at once. Make small goals so you can achieve

them! You gain momentum this way. You know what I did with that sweet potato I worked out with? Yep, you guessed it: I ate it! It's good for you and it tastes good going down. "Healthy" doesn't mean bad tasting, at all. It may be different than what you're used to, too, but give it a try and you will see how much better you feel, think, and act each day! I came from Mississippi where butter is a main ingredient for EVERYTHING. So instead of using butter, I use coconut oil. It's so much better for you and it makes the food taste amazing. Small adjustments here and there add up, just like pennies. You keep putting those pennies in a jar and eventually they will add up to a nice vacation. Well, you keep putting healthy food in your body little by little and before you know it, you've added a few years to your life.

You may ask what does food have to do with alcohol or drugs? Nothing, except that the alcohol and drugs I put in my body for so long were poisons and put me in a bad place mentally, physically, and emotionally. There's so much I don't know scientifically about how the foods have such an effect on your body, but I do know from experience how I feel after I eat a banana versus how I feel after I eat a candy bar. The energy from the banana is constant and seems to be just the right amount that I need, whereas the candy bar gets me all hyped up for a while, but then it dies off and I feel so tired and just blah. I'm still so intrigued with this whole food thing. It really blows my mind how the pieces are all connected to each other.

I have even cut red meat out of my diet now. I eat it on very rare occasions, and every single time I do I get so dad-gum sleepy, I can't keep my eyes open. And I used to eat steaks for every meal, if I had the chance. Not anymore. All I'm saying, Lil Babies, is you are worth taking care of your body. You deserve this! All great things take work. You won't change all your eating habits overnight. I'm not even trying to suggest that. I want this to be a new lifestyle for you, not just some diet you try for 30 days and then go right back to your old ways. Baby step your way to the greatest version of you in all areas. That's what this whole book is about.

⭐ *Get 'er done:*

> *Focus on changing one thing at a time. Make a list of all the foods and drinks you want to change. Then make a separate list of the foods and drinks that you can replace them with. Start at the top of the list and master replacing that bad food or drink with a good food or drink. Once you mastered that one, move on to the next item on your list. And keep going until you eventually have mastered all of the foods and drinks on your list.*

Walk or Run Outside to Observe Nature

Nature is one of the most amazing things ever. There are so many life lessons to be learned, as long as you're open to receive them. Taking a walk or run, even if it's just around the block, can offer you such peace of mind and it's also good for the body. I know what you're thinking: "You want me to do what? Run?" Haha. Trust me when I tell you that this was the absolutely hardest step in this whole book for me to get down pat. For as long as I was in my addiction, I also smoked cigarettes and the thought of running sounded cute, but the whole process wasn't cute at all.

When I found a new clan to hang out with, they were really into the whole running thing, so of course, I had to step it up a notch and join them. I promise you I couldn't even run a quarter of a mile at first without stopping 5 times. I couldn't breathe and I felt like I was going to die. I got so mad that I couldn't breathe, I kicked the cigarettes, too. They kept telling me to keep at it, it will get better. My knees felt like they needed WD-40 to operate right. I felt like they weren't going to bend and I was going to fall flat on my face. But I kept at it, just like they told me. I ran around my block so many times in tears. I just couldn't understand how they loved running. So, one day I decided to go running by the ocean. I absolutely love the ocean! For the first time since I had attempted to run, I did it!! I ran without thinking about my knees or not being able to breathe because I was so consumed with the nature around me.

I watched the birds fly over the water and then dive down in an attempt to catch a fish. It blew my mind how they could do that. The thought of the birds flying, period, was blowing my mind. Watching the waves in the water and how they splashed against the rock amazed me, too. Now it wasn't even about the running; it was about learning to love the simple things in life— the things that happen around us all day every day that most of us ignore. When you can appreciate the simple things in life, you learn to see beauty in everything and in everyone. Now my focus wasn't on the problem (running), but was on the solution (nature) instead.

Not only is it amazing, but something about being outside and listening to all the natural noises is soothing. It reminds you that you are living in a world that's so much bigger than you can ever imagine. Life is so complex, but so simple at the same time. I don't know about you, but when I'm out in nature, I get so intrigued. How does the wind even make the trees blow around? How do these wild animals know what to do? What makes the waves crash over the rocks? It takes my mind to a place that I don't get to experience when I'm running around like a chicken with my head cut off. It forces me to explore parts of my mind that have dust on them. We all are guilty of just going through the motions of life. Get up, go to work at the same old job, doing the same old thing, driving the same old way to and from, cooking the same old meals, going to bed at the same old time... and we rarely live life. We don't stop and admire the amazing beauty of much of anything because we are scared we will miss something if our routine gets out of whack, when the reality is that we're missing out on life's most priceless and valuable lessons.

Have you ever sat down and watched ants? They are probably the most annoying little critters out there. They seem to take over everything so quick, but they are so amazing. You want to talk about being in a clan that supports each other? That's the ants. They help each other carry food. Sometimes they are all in a line and one of the ants seems to go down the line and high five the other ones, like it's saying, "Good job, Buddy!" They gather up food and store it for the winter together. They rarely do things alone. They exemplify teamwork. One day, when you need to get some of that alone time in, go outside and put a piece of food down for the ants to carry and watch all the magic happen. It will blow your mind how something so small can be so smart.

Go pick up a random rock and sit there and observe the colors in it. Your mind will start to think about how all the colors came to be in there. And though you may not have the answer right then, it may just make you want to do more research on that bad boy, which will be feeding your mind with knowledge. Win-win! Things that you normally used to take for granted will now become beautiful to you. Anytime I feel frustrated, if it's where I can do so in that moment, I go outside, take a walk, and just look around. I can't really explain it, but it always brings me back to a place of gratitude and peace. Every single time. Honestly, it's not just about the activity of running or walking—which is great (don't get me wrong) and super important, so you can take good care of your body—but the mental clarity you get from being outside is indescribable. This is definitely something you will have to experience for yourself to understand exactly what I'm talking about.

Go find a trail of some sort in your area, take a walk/run on it, and soak it all in. You don't have to start off running (like me), but if you're looking to quit smoking, that's a surefire way to do it. Watch the plants and the critters around you! Watch how they move through life and I promise, you will be amazed, too!

🕐 *Get 'er done:*

Start small, by taking a 5-minute walk/run every day outside. Quiet your mind and look around you. Find one thing in nature that sparks your interest and think about how it operates.

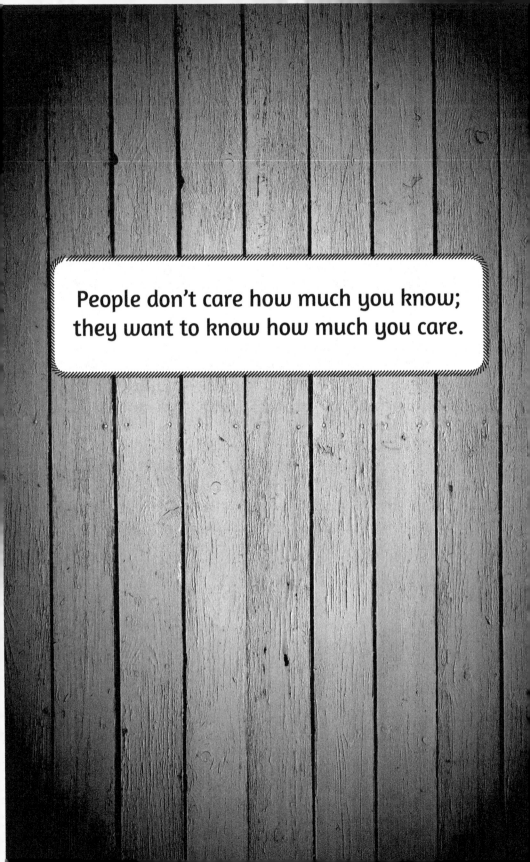

People don't care how much you know;
they want to know how much you care.

CONTINUOUSLY MAKE A STRANGER SMILE

Encourage 3 People Daily

Have you ever gotten a random text or phone call from someone that just wanted to tell you to have a good day? My heart smiles so big when I receive one unexpectedly. You have the power to change someone's life. It's up to you to decide to change it for the good or change it for the bad. Somehow, along the way we have lost touch with connecting with others. And I mean *really* connecting, not just giving someone a like or a comment on Facebook or Instagram. I mean going that extra little mile to find something about them and connect with them on that. We are all so critical of each other, and I don't understand why that has to be. If we all worked together and helped each other, this world would be a much more beautiful place to live in. Again, we get so caught up in the same old routines that we forget that others around are sometimes struggling or sometimes celebrating small wins. I need you to be their personal cheerleader. Okay, so you don't have to go full cheerleader mode, but I want you to start being aware of the folks that are in your life.

I don't know how it works out this way, but almost 100% of the time when I send these simple messages to people, they come back saying, "Wow! I really needed that today." It blows my mind how God places it in my heart which people to reach out to. People don't care how much you know; they want to know how much you care. Look around you today. Maybe there's a coworker that you don't really like. For whatever reason, this person has rubbed you the wrong way. Find a strength in them. What's one thing they do well? You got it? Now go tell them. And tell them with a smile on your face or send them an email or text. Did you do it? I bet they were a little shocked that you did, but I bet you made their day. That wasn't so bad, was it?

Becoming aware of others really opens up so many doors to feed your soul some goodness. Even though the whole point of encouraging people is to help them have a better day, something about being able to put a smile on someone else's face touches your own soul. Win-win! The more you do this, the more you will be able to tell who needs a smile the most. Remember, everyone is seeking love and acceptance. Sometimes the ones that seem so harsh are the exact ones who need that love and acceptance the most. Everyone is going through something. Everyone has things in their life that they are dealing with. You aren't the only one. You trying to kick a habit is so amazing and it takes a lot of hard work, but you aren't the only person in this world. It's not always about YOU! Just like it's not always about me.

As humans, we need each other to thrive. We can survive by ourselves, but when you want to reach the level of true happiness, you have to have other humans around. You have to add value to their lives, just like they have to add value to yours. It's a constant motion. Again, I'm no expert on any of this kind of stuff; I'm just doing my very best to explain what I've come to know to be true. I have gone days and days in my sobriety where I was feeling down on myself, but I wasn't even putting into practice my own principles of making others smile. My justification was: "I'm not feeling amazing today, so how can I possibly help anyone else feel amazing today?" One day it dawned on me that this is exactly how I can feel amazing again. Humans have a natural instinct to help others, just like a herd of animals. We want to nurture and be nurtured. Somewhere along the line though, that need for nurturing got disturbed. We stopped caring whether we actually gave it out or took it in. This to me has played a huge role in the reason I stayed so long in my addiction. I didn't feel loved and because I didn't know that giving love out to others could help me, I chose to fill that void with substances that just made matters worse.

I just got accepted to Penn State University, where I will be studying Human Development and Family Studies so I can gain further knowledge on all of this. I can't wait to dive in, because I feel deep in my soul that the way humans communicate and treat each other plays a big role in how humans decide to live their life. Start speaking life into everyone you see. You just may be the very person that saves their life. Be kind to one another.

Start with people at your workplace or some folks in your new clan. My messages are super simple. I may send, "Hey, hey, hey!! I hope you have an amazing day!" When I said simple, I meant really simple. I don't think it's so much *what* you say to folks; I think it's the fact that you thought of them that brings a smile to their face. Once you've made someone smile, I can't even describe the feeling inside it creates for you. Not only are you empowering someone else; you're also empowering yourself! Happy people are happy because they make others happy. I just need you to do it so you can understand what I mean.

♥ *Get 'er done:*

> *Be that light for someone today. Send an encouraging text or email to 3 people a day. Something super simple can make someone's day so much brighter.*

Speak to Everyone Within 10 Feet

In my opinion, our society has gotten so consumed with our cell phones and social media that we don't even notice real live people around us anymore. We are more concerned about what is happening across the country in another state than with what's going on right in front of us, in our eye's view. It's hard to remember sometimes, but there was a time when the technology wasn't as advanced and we had to speak to each other in person. I'm not at all knocking technology. I think it's amazing, but in my life, I try to keep it old school as much as possible. Everywhere I go, I make it a point to say "Hey! How are you?" and smile to everyone within 10 feet of me. Most of the time it takes people by surprise, but they almost always respond back! Smiles are simple, they're free, and they're super contagious!

Every chance I get, I leave my phone in the car when I go to the grocery store or to the gas station. One of my biggest pet peeves is when someone is at the cash register paying and they are talking on the phone, especially if it's a situation where conversation between the customer and cashier must take place and then they ignore the cashier because they are so consumed with the phone conversation. I am speaking from experience. Back in Mississippi, I helped my dad manage his convenience stores for a while. In my opinion, it's rude and insensitive to the one trying to give good customer service. Trust me, I understand that there are emergencies and phone calls that have to be taken, but a lot of them can wait for a few minutes until you can pay for your items, speak to the person giving you good service, and leave the store. I told you I'm old school. The thing is we have to get back to this place of awareness of others... just being conscious that others are around us.

People don't feel special when you walk up to the counter and bark at them while you're on the phone with someone else. That's not a way any of us accomplish anything. I'm not saying you have to carry on a 15-minute conversation with everyone you come in contact with (that would make it impossible to get anything done), but what I am asking you to do is simply speak to everyone. Smile ever so genuine and say, "Good morning." Or "Good afternoon." Or "Have an amazing day." Say something positive, just to show the slightest bit of compassion to someone. That cashier at Walmart who may be going super slow may have just experienced a death in her family. You don't ever know what someone is going through, but you can always offer a little compassion. Instead of getting angry at them for being slow, encourage them: "Hey! You're doing a great job." I'm telling you, you may just be the one that brings them out a slump. They may have just prayed to God, "Show some kind of sign for me to live today," and YOU could be that sign that keeps them alive.

Seriously, you just don't ever know. Remember, everyone is always going through something.

Just yesterday, I was at the Wally World to get some supplies to give out to the homeless people in my community. I was standing in line at the deli and behind me was an older lady. I simply turned around and said "Hey!" to her. We talked for about 5 or 10 minutes. She was telling me about how she used to feed the homeless, too, when she could, but now she's not able to. It was as if she hadn't talked to anyone that whole day and you just don't ever know, you may be the only person someone hears from during the whole week. That's crazy to think about, but it's true. Some people live such a lonely life, you may be the only sunshine in their darkness. When I got all I needed from the deli, I said goodbye to the lady. She told me her name and gave me the biggest hug ever. It made my heart smile so big. Neither one of us would have been able to get a hug if I had just stood in line and kept my mouth shut.

You may not know what to talk to people about, so when you say "hey" to them, most people want to be heard, so all you have to do is just listen. Some folks are just waiting to have that listening ear. Listening and giving someone your undivided attention are actually two of the best things you can do to show someone you care. And the good news is, neither one of those two things cost anything, except a little bit of your time. We don't all have money to spare, but we all can make time for someone else to make their day a little better. Get out of your comfort zone and speak to people everywhere you go. It truly brings an awareness of others to your life. Then, in turn, it will make *your* life more fulfilling.

☆ *Get 'er done:*

> *I challenge you to leave your cell phone in the car every time you go to Walmart or the grocery store. Say "HEY" to everyone within 10 feet of you and even throw a compliment to someone. You'll be glad you did.*

Do Something Special for Someone Every Day

My life song and dance is "Make a Stranger Smile." I just believe that, if we all made at least one person happy each day, before long we could turn this whole world around. Imagine if everyone you came in contact with was joyful and living life to the fullest, helping each other along the way. How amazing would that be? I could write a book on examples of how me and my daughter have made strangers smile, but the crazy thing is that, in doing this, it makes *my* day 10 times better. Every day I ask God to send me somebody to help. He never fails to send them. I just have to make sure I'm obedient and help the people he's sent.

Most people are so selfish and only have themselves in their vision. I really can't stress this enough. Every person on this earth wants to be loved and accepted. Everyone! It doesn't matter what kind of life you lived or what your neighbor has been through; ultimately, we all want the same thing. Being able to make someone's day is a power that all of us possess. You have the power to change someone's life through the smallest gestures.

This is my most favorite thing to do. I love being able to make someone smile. I love making someone feel super special. I know what it's like to be called worthless and feel like the whole world was against me. Maybe this is why I'm so passionate about helping others feel worthy. It's a horrible feeling that I wouldn't wish on anyone. I go out of my way every single day to make someone's day a little brighter. Some days it costs me a little money, and other days it doesn't, but the smile on their face is priceless and can't be bought with any amount of money.

Here are my top two favorites so far...

1. After my car got repossessed and right before I got evicted from my apartment, I decided to go for a run with my puppy dog. I saw someone digging in the dumpster, but before I realized what I had seen, I had passed it by a couple of feet. I stopped dead in my tracks and went back without hesitation. I met the most amazing woman—Nanny, from South America. She was all dirty from digging in the dumpster and I asked her if she was hungry. I told her I'd just got done cooking and I would be more than happy to go get her a plate of food. She said she would love some, and asked me if there was any way I could get her some milk. I knew I only had a few dollars (I literally had about $15 to my name), but I had what I needed to survive at that moment, so I ran back to my apartment, put the pup up, made her a plate of food, and stopped by the dollar store to get a gallon of milk for her. I didn't have much to offer her, but I shared what I had. She waited for me on a bench with all her treasures she'd found in the dumpster. I helped her carry all her bags of stuff back to an alley, where she was staying in someone's garage. We talked the whole way there! She was smiling from ear to ear. I hung out with her for a little bit and when I went to leave,

she gave me the biggest hug ever! When I was on my way back to my apartment, tears of joy were streaming down my face because I knew she had some food for the night and a smile in her heart. I think the time I spent with her was more important than the gallon of milk or the food I gave her. She just wanted to feel loved.

2. On the day I got evicted, I got my car back and I promised God that I would use it to help folks that didn't have one. There was a bus stop right in front of the hotel I was staying in and one morning, while taking my puppy dog for a walk, I saw a man standing there. I could tell he had some sort of animal with him and a couple of bags. I spoke to him and got the impression he was having a rough day. He told me that the day before, he was on the bus and left his wallet on it and he was trying to get to the main bus station. I asked him if he needed a ride and you would have thought I'd offered him a million dollars. I put my dog up and met him back at my car, where we introduced ourselves. (I always make sure God tells me who to put in my car and who not to put in my car. Don't worry, I'm super careful!) Harry and his cat loaded up in my car and off to the bus station we went. I offered to buy him breakfast, but he said he wasn't hungry. The crazy thing was he'd just gotten evicted, too, and was trying to get to a relative's house.

We pulled up at the main bus station and he went in to locate his wallet. He came out all lit up like a Christmas tree because all of his belongings were intact. I offered to drive him the extra couple miles to the relative's house and he so thankfully agreed. I got the opportunity to speak life into him and give him some hope while we were driving. When we got to his destination, I asked him if he would mind if I prayed with him. This grown man broke down in tears and said no one in his whole life had ever been so generous. I gave him a hug and told him everything was going to be okay and gave him all the cash I had on me—$40. I gave him my number in case he needed anything at all and a few days later, I received a text from him, saying that he was so thankful for the kind act and that I had saved his life by giving him a ride. I know I made that stranger smile that day, but it wasn't about what I *did* for him; it was just the fact that I cared enough to help him. What he doesn't know is that he changed *my* life by allowing me to help him.

I'm not sharing these stories to boast about what I've done for people, but to give you examples of how you can make an impact on someone's life just by being aware that they exist. Just by taking a few extra minutes out of your day to help someone who may not have any other way. Folks, you don't have to spend any money on anyone to make them feel special. Most of the time folks just want to know you care. They want to feel loved. Go hug someone. Go hold the door for someone. Listen to a complete stranger for a little while. The opportunities to make someone feel special are endless, but the feeling that you get inside yourself from helping someone is priceless. All *your* problems go away because you created a solution for someone else.

♥ *Get 'er done:*

Look around at all the places you go for a need you can fill. Ask God to send you someone you can be a blessing to and be on the lookout for them. Sit and talk with a stranger, give a rose to a random person, buy the items for the person behind you in line at the convenience store, etc. There's always someone somewhere that needs a smile Please be that person for them.

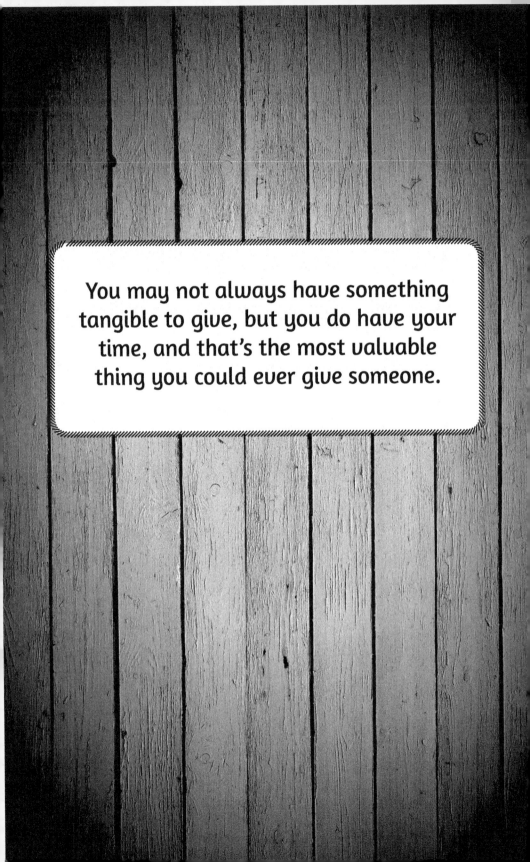

You may not always have something tangible to give, but you do have your time, and that's the most valuable thing you could ever give someone.

THROW OUT HELP

Be a Giver

I once heard a wise man say, "Not everything you get is yours to keep." Meaning, sometimes you will get blessed with something, monetary or not, and it's intended for you to give it to someone in need. For instance, someone may give you a gift card to a local restaurant but God will send someone in your path for you to pass that gift card to them. Giving people are the happiest people around. Folks think because they don't have a lot of money to give to big charities that they shouldn't give at all. I promise you, every little bit helps, especially to someone that has nothing. You may not always have something tangible to give, but you do have your time, and that's the most valuable thing you could ever give someone.

I started taking food to some homeless folks in a park downtown. I tried to do it every couple of days, but this particular day I didn't have any extra funds to buy anything. I remembered I had a small empty notebook, so I grabbed it and a pen and headed down to that park. On the way to the park, I thought about what I could do with this notebook that would be giving value to them. And I came up with something. I'm not going to lie. At first I had doubts running through my head: "What if they see me coming and expect me to have something in my hands to give them?" And then, "What would I say if they asked me for that something I couldn't give them?" But I had to put all those doubts aside and not worry about the things I can't control.

Once I got there, I walked over to a bench where a few of them were sitting, took out my notebook, and started talking to them about their dreams. I asked them this question: "If money wasn't an issue where or what would you be doing right now?" They started naming off some things, so I had them each write it down in that notebook and then tear the page off and hang on to it to look at when they felt like giving up. I ended up spending an hour with some amazing people. It turns out they didn't want anything from me, except to know I care. They never asked me for anything. No money, no food. Just hanging out with someone is exactly what they needed to keep them going.

Now let me share a lesson with you that I learned, which changed my life forever. Once you start helping others and making them smile, you have to be open to receiving that same kindness. You can't always give, give, give. Your cup has to be replenished, too. You can't deny others trying to help you, because if you do, you are depriving them of being able to feel good on the inside. Basically, you are depriving them of happiness and we don't want anyone unhappy. In order to keep the cycle going, you have to give in order to receive and you have to receive in order to give. Your heart must be open to both. Remember, we are in the business of making folks happy, so don't ever rob someone of that opportunity.

For so long, I thought I could do everything by myself and I didn't need any help. All I wanted to do was to help people and I didn't know that, in order for me to continue to do that, I had to receive as well. Once I started learning more about myself, it wasn't that I didn't think I *needed* help, but it was I didn't feel like I *deserved* help. I didn't feel worthy of receiving what others were offering to me. This is why it's so important to speak life into yourself, to forgive yourself, and to believe in yourself. This whole book is a constant moving circle. You need all the components to live a happy life and they all tie into each other just like Mind, Body, and Soul. They all complement the others. If one aspect is missing, they can't connect properly. It's super important that you know your worth and you know how much you deserve in this world, so you can freely give that same concept out to others in this world.

Everywhere you go, ask yourself "How can I add value to the people around me?" Everyone has a different level of value they can add in every different situation. Some folks can make others smile, some folks can give out money, some folks can offer rides, some folks can offer services... you get my point. Everyone is at different levels in life, but everyone has something to offer. Don't get caught up in comparing yourself to how much the next person gave. You concentrate on what *you* can give people.

You may have some old clothes you've been meaning to sell in a garage sale. Why don't you just give them to someone that may not have as many clothes as you do? Or maybe you have only $1.00 to give to someone for bus fare. Maybe you can offer to babysit for a friend to give them a date night. I want you to get in the habit of finding needs and filling them.

💜 *Get 'er done:*

> *In every relationship you are in, always ask how you can add value. Look around everywhere you go and find ways to add value to strangers, but remember, in order to keep your cup full and not to deprive someone else of their duties, you must also openly receive. Practice allowing people to help YOU!*

Volunteer

Be of service to people without expecting anything in return. Always look for a need, everywhere you go, and fill it. Think about the things you're most passionate about and look for opportunities to volunteer in that area. That way you get more satisfaction out of it because it's doing things you love doing. There are always so many ways to serve in your community.

I absolutely love watching folks train for Ninja Warrior-type events. My friends had a competition at their gym (kind of like a mini-Ninja Warrior) where some of the best of the best in Florida were going to be there. I couldn't wait to go watch them. If you don't know anything about Ninja Warrior, it's an obstacle course designed to test agility, speed, and upper body strength. Some of these men and women make it look incredibly easy, but I know from personal humbling experience, it's definitely not as easy as they make it look. It takes so much time and effort to train for.

Instead of just watching on the sidelines like most people do, I asked them to put me to work. My job was to make sure the rings were back in place at a particular obstacle so the next opponent could breeze right on through. In my mind, it was a small job, but if you look at the whole big picture, all the small jobs like that make the whole course flow smoothly. Not only did I get to watch the event, but I played a small role in helping these amazing athletes complete the course with no interruption. And that's a HUGE deal. It's a lot of work putting something like that together. I don't think volunteering is just about making you feel good, but it gives you a deeper awareness for all the hard work involved in creating an event. When you sit on the sidelines and are just a spectator, you don't fully understand the level of effort it takes to make it look the way it does.

There are tons of volunteer opportunities in your city. It takes a whole army to put together anything amazing. Maybe you love animals and can volunteer at your local humane society. You may be the pooper scooper, but without you, those Lil Babies would be rolling around playing in their own poop. And that's just nasty. There's no job too small to help with. Every single job is a puzzle piece in the big picture. Ya'll know how puzzles work. It doesn't start off amazing. It doesn't even remotely look like the picture on the box until you start putting more and more pieces together. It's the same way in real life.

I didn't necessarily think that things just magically happened, but I honestly didn't have any awareness of all the hard work people put into things, because my awareness for others was nonexistent. I was selfish, so I never saw past myself. When you truly get that awareness of others down pat and sincerely want to lend yourself in any way possible, it's like seeing life through a completely different lens. You will begin to see all the hard work it takes; you will begin to see the importance of all the little jobs. You may not think a small role is a big deal, but I guarantee you, it is.

I used to be that person who always just sat and watched, but not anymore. It doesn't matter if it's a small get-together with family or a huge event I attend, I will always offer to help in some way, because no matter how big or small the task you are assigned, it takes hard work to accomplish everything. Helping someone else accomplish their goals or dreams is an indescribable feeling. You could be the missing puzzle piece to make that masterpiece for someone.

💜 *Get 'er done:*

Look for volunteer opportunities in your community. Someone needs YOU to help make their dreams come true. Volunteer somewhere twice a month; you'll be glad you did.

Share a Story of a Struggle with Someone

I don't know why we are all so scared letting people see us fall. We all fall at some point in our lives. I know I have—over and over and over again, too many times to count. If we never fall, we can never learn to be successful in anything. I started being super transparent and letting folks see my failures so that they could know if they ever come up against the same thing, they also can make it through it, just like I did. I want to give hope to folks that can't see a way out of their situation. That's the reason I'm writing this book in the first place. While I was going through the car repossession and eviction, a time when I was hurting the most and feeling like a failure, my mentor told me, "Everything you go through isn't about you. Sometimes you will experience something so that you can show compassion to others on a deeper level when they go through those same things." When I heard this, it changed my life forever. Because you went through certain things, now you will be able to offer hope to so many people where others won't be able to help. Looking back on all the things I've been through in my life that (when they happened) I couldn't understand why I had to experience them, now it all makes perfect sense. IT'S NOT EVEN ABOUT ME. When I changed my mindset, it made sharing a struggle easier, because now I know it's going to set someone free.

There are days on my journey when I cry and I get frustrated, but then I have to look back to see how much I've already overcome. There were times when the power got turned off; there were times when I didn't know how I was going to feed my child; there were times when I didn't know where I was going to sleep. But I just kept pressing forward. There were days when I didn't have the energy to keep going, but I did it anyways. There are days when I want to throw my hands up in the air with my teenage daughter and push her off on someone else, but then I remember she's the only biological daughter I will ever be able to have anymore. I had a tubal pregnancy in my addiction, my tube ruptured, I had internal bleeding, and had to have emergency surgery. Four months after that, I had another miscarriage. I firmly believe I wasn't intended to have any more children in those years because I wasn't being the best mom to the one I had. I ended up having a hysterectomy because of so many complications and now I won't get that opportunity again to birth another child, so I keep striving to be the best mom I can possibly be. For a while, I was mad at God for everything that I went through, but now I know that because I went through so much, I can help that many more people overcome their own struggles.

Everything you go through in life has a lesson attached to it. Your job is to learn the lesson and then be able to reach back and grab someone else's hand to help them through the same storm. How are we supposed to help others if we can't be vulnerable and share the things we've been through? I'm not saying you have to share every little bitty detail of your life, but I am saying that talking about some of the hardest lessons you've learned or some of the hardest experiences you've made it through—those are the types of things that will be able to help someone.

I started sharing my story of addiction very early on, probably within the first few weeks of my new life. I started small and shared some of it with a few select people that I knew wouldn't judge me. So, when I was led to put it on Facebook and then start making a YouTube channel about the things I'd dealt with, I did go to these people to advise me on what I should do. None of them said, "Go for it." A few of them said I should share it privately to people I wanted to help. But in order to get my message out into the world and help as many people as I could, I had to go with my gut and just share. I didn't know how people would react. It was a scary thing to do at first, but I always stayed honest and true to myself and the values I placed in my life. I didn't realize how much I freed my own self by trying to help others. I'm telling you, every chapter in this book is a win-win for everyone—for you and for the people you will help along the way!

Be authentic. Don't tell the things you know that people would like to hear. Give them the good, the bad, and the ugly. I just believe that the only way people will truly learn and truly get hope is by your being truthful. Have the right intentions behind it when you share your struggles. Don't share just to get attention, but share in order to be that guiding light through a dark tunnel. People are waiting for YOU to help them. There's someone right now that needs to hear your story, to give them that motivation to keep going. They may feel like giving up. They may feel like ending their life, but YOU could be the very person that keeps them alive, just by sharing how you came out of the dark valley.

⏰ *Get 'er done:*

> *Sit down and write out a struggle that you've been through. Think of someone you may know that is experiencing the same kind of thing and reach out to them. Share your testimony of how God helped you through that storm. Give them that hope they desperately need.*

> ## It's super important that you know your worth and you know how much you deserve in this world, so you can freely give that same concept out to others in this world.

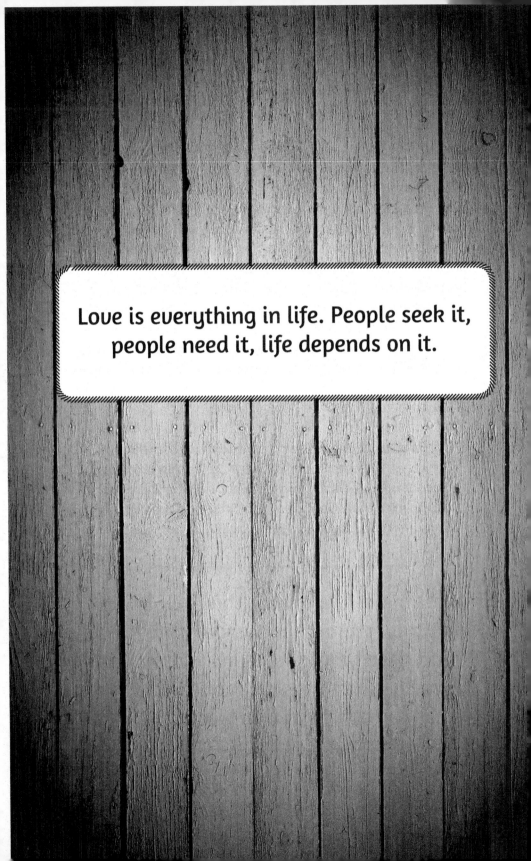

Love is everything in life. People seek it, people need it, life depends on it.

PUTTING IT ALL TOGETHER

There you have it, folks. Those are the principles that changed my life. Applying these principles daily allowed me to get from being a broken, addicted girl who felt absolutely worthless to the place I'm at today, where I love life. Each day I wake up, I am so grateful. I don't take it for granted, like I used to. I didn't grow overnight and you can't expect to either. All good things take time to mold. Apply one principle at a time and once you've read the whole book, go back and read it again and again until all the principles become a habit. The ultimate goal is to create new habits that replace the old ones. I'm not going to sugar coat this for you: you *will* have hard days. You will experience pain. You will get tired. You will be joyful. You will happy dance. But what you CANNOT do is ever give up.

If I saw you today, I would tell you to your face, "If I can do this, so can you! You're worth it!" I never in a million years imagined my life as it is now. I never thought for one second, after all the things I'd done and all the people I hurt, that I would be able to live a happy life. I didn't know I was allowed to get another chance. And the crazy thing is that I was seriously thinking about ending it all one day. Wow! I'm so thankful I didn't. I thank God every single day for allowing me to see the opportunity to live again. I thank God for chance after chance to be able to get it right. I don't always know the right things to do or the right moves to make, but I do wake up each day striving to be a better person than I was yesterday, and that's all anyone can hope for.

You may be thinking, "That's great, Amanda, but you don't know what all I've done and you don't understand." True, I don't know what all you've been through, but I do know that it doesn't even matter what you've done or who you've hurt; there is opportunity today for a new life. I do know that no matter what anyone says; you deserve the chance to live life. I know first-hand that addiction is very tiring. I know that it causes damage on so many different levels. There are so many different kinds of addictions out there, but ultimately, they are all the same. They are all filling some sort of void and you now have a guideline on how to fill that void with goodness. Eventually, all the pain that you feel will go away.

I'm no expert at any of this and a lot of what I've written I can't explain scientifically, but I did live it, so I speak from experience. What life has taught me is that you can find a lesson in everything. There are no failures as long as you keep going. You only fail if you quit. You may feel like life is beating you down right now, but the reality is life is always going to test you. The solution is to change your mindset. Two different people can go through the same circumstance and have two totally different outcomes because of the way they perceive the situation. Life has taught me that there's beauty in everything. There's a beauty in brokenness, there's beauty in the unknown, there's beauty in all the pain you've experienced. Love is everything in life. People seek it, people need it, life depends on it. Life is always changing, it's just up to you if you want to accept the change and take a leap of faith to live a life you've always known you should live.

Everything we do and everything we are is based on what we think about. Whether you see yourself as a King/Queen or whether you see yourself as a loser is ultimately up to you. I think you've experienced the loser role for too dad-gum long. It's time to get your life back. It's time to try new things because the things you've done for so long haven't gotten you the results you truly desire. You aren't alone anymore. I am now your personal cheerleader and I'm looking forward to hearing about your success story.

Connecting Mind, Body, and Soul is imperative to living a happy, vibrant, SOBER life. You can't have one without the other. You have to work them all daily. Connecting to love, connecting to your purpose, connecting back to YOU is the key to beating this thing. Taking baby steps each day will guide you on your new path. It's not easy, but if it were easy, everyone would be doing it. Because you're reading this book, you've already taken steps that others haven't taken. Give yourself a hug from me because you are going to beat this thing. I have no doubts in my mind. I believe in you, Lil Babies!

When you look at the whole big picture of all the things you have to change in order to live the life you've always wanted, it's overwhelming. It's a whole lifestyle change. You can't just fix something for 30 days and expect it to be cured. You have to work at this thing every single day. It has to become part of your routine in order to get the results you are looking for. I'm telling you this, because no one told *me* when I went to rehab.

No one told me that I was going to have to work at this the rest of my life. I promise you, though, it's *so* worth it. Eventually these new habits will become something you don't even have to make yourself do; you will just do them because your Mind, Body, and Soul will crave them. This doesn't mean you won't face life. Life is going to try it's best to beat you down, but since you've been practicing building your inner strength muscles and learning who to lean on, you can make it through anything. Just say to yourself, *"I can do ALL things through Christ who gives me strength."* (Philippians 4:13)

When you feel like giving up, think about why you started in the first place. Think about the people that are most important to you, the ones that you are doing this for. They want to see you happy and live life to the fullest. Use these principles as a guideline every day. When you combine them with your amazing will power, BECAUSE YOU AREN'T GOING TO GIVE UP, you are about to experience life in a way you've never seen it before. You are about to find that love you've always been searching for.

You are so much stronger than you think!

PATCHED WANGS

When I moved away from Mississippi, I never had any intentions of going back. Never. But the more I thought about it, I came to realize that I was being totally selfish, because ALL of my family is there. There's no way I could live my life and never go see any of them. When I did visit, I just didn't know it would be so soon. My dad asked if we could come back home for Christmas and I promise you, I tried to come up with every excuse in the book. I realized, though, it wasn't about going to see my family at all, but I had only been gone for about 7 months and I wasn't sure if I was strong enough to stay away from the people, places, and things that I had moved to get away from. The thought of getting stuck back in that trap again scared the crap out of me. It was a huge fear of mine. Not only that, but there was a pending felony I was still dealing with and I was scared to make a wrong move and end up back in jail.

I had to remember all the things I'd been learning about and all the principles I'd put into play for myself. I couldn't believe one thing and then live my life a totally different way. That's called being a hypocrite, and I surely didn't want to put that vibe out into the world anymore. I have been learning that facing your fears and overcoming them is the only way you can grow.

Sometimes we make such a big deal about things in our mind, we make the thing itself worse than it really is, so we keep putting it off. But then, when we actually *accomplish* that thing, it doesn't seem so bad at all. The mind is so very powerful. I decided to put all my feelings and fears aside and just go back home to spend a few days with my family.

On the drive there, I wanted to turn around so many times. My heart started beating fast and my palms were sweating as I crossed that Mississippi line. I had to look at myself in my visor mirror so many times and tell myself, "Girl, you got this! Calm down, everything is going to be okay." We had an awesome Christmas with my family. The feeling I got when I rode by certain places and saw certain people was really strange. I could feel I didn't belong there in that city or with those people. (Not that there's anything wrong with either of them, but my home was now in Florida.) But I was reminded just where I came from, and all the pain associated with that gave me all the motivation I needed to go back to Florida and chase what they call a dream. Even though (at that time) I didn't know what that dream entailed for me, I knew I wanted to help folks that felt like I had for so long.-Worthless, hopeless, depressed, and lonely. It's really strange, but even though I was finally in a good place, I could tell that all those emotions were associated with this place, like I kind of felt them trying to creep in on me.

One night, lying in bed, in the very place that caused me so much pain, I asked God what I was supposed to do with all of this. I mean, how was I supposed to turn all of this into helping people? I'd never done anything like this before and had no idea where to start or what I would call it. It's a beautiful thing when you start to learn how to talk and listen to God. I heard plain as day, "Patched Wangs."

I thought, "What in the world am I supposed to do with that? It doesn't even make sense to me." I tried to come up with different names, but nope, this one was it. And the only sense I could make out of it is this:

There was a time where I was so broken by life, I was so bruised from all the falls I made, I was scarred from all shame I felt, but somehow, I came out of it all. Somehow, I found joy again. Somehow, I learned to spread my wings and fly again. All the pain, the bruises, and the scars were healing because I was in the midst of living the solution to all my problems. What I didn't know before that moment was that the very things that were keeping me sober—the ones I thought were just common sense—were the very principles I am teaching you in this book. A light bulb went off in my brain, and immediately I started writing down all the things I'd done up until that point that had replaced my drinking or using.

Patched Wangs (for the record, I had to make wings into a country slang word, so now it's wangs) is about giving hope and direction to those who have ever felt like I did. As I was writing all these things out, in no particular order, I didn't even understand the value of them until about 10 months later. The more I learned, the more I grew, and the more I kept thinking about all these things. My mentor, Eric Thomas, kept repeating over and over and over in different spaces, "You can see certain problems, because you are the one that has the solution," meaning that, because I went through certain things in my life and now had come out on the other side of it, I can turn around and teach someone else how I did it. Brilliant. Now, God, how am I going to do that? I knew for a while that I wanted to write a book, but I honestly didn't know in what direction to take my first book. I had experienced so much and have so much to say, I was always conflicted. Ask and you shall receive.

One of my brothers from another mother, Bolaji O, came up with this amazing system of writing a book that highlighted one solution for one problem. Oh, my gosh! It was in alignment with what my mentor has been telling me for a while now. As I'm going through this process of figuring out an acronym to best describe the solution to the problem and figuring out who my target audience is, it really all came together for me and blew my mind. Everything I'd written down that changed my life is the very solution I'm going to use to change other's lives. The goal was to come up with an acronym that best described what I was trying to accomplish. When I pulled out the list I'd been making for quite some time (of all the actions I took to get sober), I realized they all connected to each other. I couldn't just do one thing from that list and be sober; it consisted of a number of things I had to do daily. They all intertwined together with each other and fed each other, so I categorized them into Mind, Body, and Soul.

C.O.N.N.E.C.T. That's it! That's my acronym! The definition of connect is: to join, link, or fasten together; unite or bind. I couldn't just work Mind and Body and be sober, just like I couldn't work only Soul and Mind and be sober. It was literally connecting all three of them together that allowed me to experience the joy and happiness I never even dreamed about having. I had no idea this kind of life existed and it made me reflect on just how much time I wasted in an unnecessary addiction because I wasn't educated on baby steps I could take.

The baby steps I took:

Completely live in faith

Only you need to believe

New clan time

Nurture that noggin

Energize your vessel

Continuously make a stranger smile

Throw out help

This is the formula that I took to get sober. This is the solution to my problem of addiction. I never felt anyone cared enough to help me through the tough days. I never thought anyone could see the diamond I was meant to be because of all the judgment I got. I want to be that person I never had. It doesn't matter how much life has beat you up. It doesn't matter how many tears you've shed. It doesn't matter how hurt you feel. You can take a breath of fresh air because you are about to get *your* wangs patched up, so YOU can fly again. You deserve this life! And I'm going to be here, cheering you on the whole way. Grab my hand and let's take this journey together!

By me facing my fears in 2015 and going back to Mississippi even when I was scared to death, something beautiful came out of it. I now have a system in place that I personally have put into play in my own life and I can teach it to you! I can testify that if you really want this thing, you can have it. If you really want happiness, you can achieve it. If you really want to be healed, you can learn to fly again just like I did.

Patched Wangs, strengthening wounded wings to fly again.

Please stay in contact with me and let me know how you're doing: amanda@patchedwangs.com

For opportunities to be coached by Amanda, please contact info@patchedwangs.com.

Find my Redneck Workouts on my website: www.patchedwangs.com

Do us both a favor and subscribe to my YouTube Channel: Patched Wangs

ABOUT THE AUTHOR

Amanda Nelson is the mother of an amazing daughter, Alexis. Together they love family runs (with their dog, Kyah) by the ocean. She is a Life Cheerleader, an Inspiration, an Ambassador of Hope, and on a mission to stop addiction, so that people can learn to make their lives be, the way God intended them to be.

CPSIA information can be obtained
at www.ICGtesting.com
Printed in the USA
LVOW13s1735180517
535011LV00011B/1054/P